Bananeras

Bananeras

*Women Transforming the Banana Unions
of Latin America*

DANA FRANK

Haymarket Books
Chicago, Illinois

Text and photographs copyright © 2005 by Dana Frank
First published in 2005 by South End Press, Cambridge, Massachusetts

This edition published in 2016 by
Haymarket Books
P.O. Box 180165
Chicago, IL 60618
773-583-7884
www.haymarketbooks.org
info@haymarketbooks.org

ISBN: 978-1-60846-535-4

Trade distribution:
In the US, Consortium Book Sales and Distribution, www.cbsd.com
In Canada, Publishers Group Canada, www.pgcbooks.ca
In the UK, Turnaround Publisher Services, www.turnaround-uk.com
All other countries, Publishers Group Worldwide, www.pgw.com

This book was published with the generous support of Lannan Foundation
and Wallace Action Fund.

Cover design by Samantha Farbman.

Printed in Canada by union labor.

Library of Congress Cataloging-in-Publication data is available.

10 9 8 7 6 5 4 3 2 1

RECYCLED
Paper made from
recycled material
FSC® C103567

Table of Contents

Rank-and-file members of SITRABI, Morales, Izabal, Guatemala, at a COSIBAH workshop on domestic violence, November 2002

To Iris Munguía

With deepest gratitude

ACKNOWLEDGMENTS

This book exists only because of the vast generosity, trust, and patience of hundreds of unionized banana workers in Latin America who welcomed me into their work and taught me how to understand it. My enormous thanks go to COLSIBA, the Coalition of Latin American Banana Unions, for such a spectacularly warm and deeply moving welcome, from that very first workshop in Guatemala City. I only hope that I can be useful in return, and that some day every banana will bear a proud union label. In Honduras, I owe my deepest gratitude to all the people who make up COSIBAH, the Coalition of Honduran Banana and Agroindustrial Unions. It's been a great privilege. Thanks for the endless hospitality, the wonderful road trips, the generous use of the office, the rides, the plantation visits, the box lunches, the jokes (including the ones I didn't get), the interviews, and so much glorious comradeship and fun. My deep thanks to Belkis Castro, Kathy Figueroa, Gloria Guzman, Claudio Hernández, Chema Martínez, Roberto Morales, Iris Munguía, Nelson Nuñez, and German Zepeda. Thank you, Zoila Lagos, in particular, for so much warmth, support, and wisdom—as well as *chisme*.

My great thanks, too, to SITRATERCO, the Union of Workers of the Tela Railroad Company, my other Honduran union family, for the warm and moving welcome, help with the project, honorary membership, and, especially, of course, the dances. Thank you Mercedes Aguilar, Oscar Amaya, Manuel Ramírez, Edgardo Rivas, and all the other dirigente/as. My special thanks to Gloria García for so much help and inspiration. In Honduras, thanks also to Mirian Reyes, Juan Funez, Oneyda Galindo, Santos Licona, Digna Figueroa, Reina Ordoñez, Gladys Briones, Nelmy Martínez, and Telma Gómez for sharing their stories and work with me. Thank you, Domitila Hernández, for the kleenex box and so much joy. Thanks, also, to the allies who helped me out: Hector Hernández, Ajax Irías, and Norma Iris Rodríguez.

Like banana women's activism, my gratitude crosses many borders. In Guatemala, thanks to Irene Barrientos, María del Carmen Molina, Petrona Savala Morales, Noé Ramírez Portela, Catalina Pérez Querra, Jesús Martínez Sosa, and Enrique Villeda (now in exile in Los Angeles). My special thanks to Selfa Sandoval Carranza, for generous help, inspiration, and poetry. Thank you Mauricio Calderon for that first tour of Guatemala City and for explaining so much. In Nicaragua, my thanks to Doris García, Mathilde Aguilar Quiroz, Gloria Reyes, and "Don Arnulfo." Thank you so much, especially, Berta Gómez, for your glorious spirit, for welcoming me into your home so full of love, and for teaching me what's really important.

In Costa Rica, thanks to Ramon Barrentos, Miriam Gómez, Ligia Lamich, Nineth Méndez, Luisa Paz, and, especially, Gilberth Bermúdez, for generous help and solidarity. Thanks from the bottom of my heart to Carlos Argüedas Mora for the hospitality, the tours, the monkeys, the coconuts, the beach, and for being such a generous soul. In Panamá, thanks to Elizabet Gonzáles and Isabel Carrasco; in Ecuador, Susana Centeno Ramírez, Edelina García, and Guillermo Touma. Last, but not least, I want to thank the incredibly brave and inspiring Colombians: Guillermo Rivera, Clara Quinto, and, especially, Adela Torres—Adela, the future is yours.

On the US side, I am equally indebted to my wonderful comrades at the US Labor Education in the Americas Project (US/LEAP), whose example, constant support, and incredibly impressive solidarity work sustained me throughout this project. I can't begin to express my admiration and gratitude. Special thanks to Joan Axthelm for the initial conversations, Gloria Vicente for the recipe, and Allison Paul for day-to-day friendship and solidarity. My thanks to Bob Perillo, in Guatemala, for generous research help as well as comradeship and advice. I also want to thank additional allies on the US and European side (broadly defined) who helped me out along the way: Liz O'Connor, Carol Pier, Jesper Nielsen, Alistair Smith, Liz Parker, and my student, Max Krochmal.

I want to thank, as well, so many scholarly friends and comrades who invited me to speak, gave me advice, and helped me out, especially those who welcomed me so warmly and respectfully as a newcomer to writing about Latin America. My thanks to Sonia

Álvarez, Gabriella Arrendondo, Raul Fernández, Jonathan Fox, Rosa-Linda Fregoso, Toni Gilpin, Gilbert Gonzáles, Emily Honig, Ruth Milkman, Priscilla Murolo, Marysa Navarro, Annelise Orleck, Aimee Schreck, Helen Shapiro, Lynn Stephen, and David Sweet. I am particularly grateful to Aviva Chomsky, Hank Frundt, and Steve Striffler for sharing unpublished work with me and welcoming me into the scholarly study of banana workers. My great thanks to Tanalís Padilla and Lisbeth Haas for reading the entire manuscript and helping make it so much better, as well as the pleasure of their friendships.

I am honored to be published by South End Press and to be part of its tradition of activist publishing. Thank you all for believing in this book, for your support for a Spanish-language edition, and for making it accessible to ordinary people. My special thanks to Asha Tall for the first-round support and to Jocelyn Burrell for support along the way; to Elizabeth Elsas, for once again giving me an amazing cover; to the proofreaders, Erich Strom and Esther Dwinell; and, most of all, to Alexander Dwinell, my editor, for such great advice and support at every turn. It's been a pleasure. Thanks, too, to Anita Palathingal and Steve Fraser at *New Labor Forum* for the article version. My thanks to Paco Ramírez, my union brother, for help with Spanish-to-English translations; and Sara Smith for help on the index. This book is currently being translated into Spanish by Janeth Blanco, in Honduras; I am grateful for the honor of working with her, and with Isolda Arita at Editorial Guaymuras.

This book was made possible in part by generous grants from the National Endowment for the Humanities, the University of California, Santa Cruz Academic Senate Committee on Research, and the University of California Institute for Labor and Employment, to all of which I am deeply grateful. My thanks also to Victor Schiffrin for scanning photographs. I also want to thank the History Department at UCSC for its support and friendship, especially Meg Lilienthal, Stephanie Hinkle, and Tim Guichard.

On the home front and beyond, thanks to many friends, loved ones, and colleagues for keeping my heart warm, my head clear, and my eyes on the prize: Frank Bardacke, Cheri Brooks, Anne Callahan, Nancy Chen, Sami Chen, Adriana Craciun, Gerri Dayharsh, Clare Delano, Eleanor Engstrand, Miriam Frank (no relation!), Marge Frantz, Julie Greene, Beth Haas, Hamsa Heinrich, Desma Holcomb, Julie Jacobs, Ann Kingsolver, Nelson Lichtenstein, John Logan, Stephen McCabe, Becky Dayharsh McCabe, Ramona Dayharsh McCabe, Wendy Mink, Amy Newell, Paul Ortiz, Sheila Payne, Thomas Pistole, Mary Beth Pudup, Katie Quan, Gerda Ray, Karin Stallard, and Alice Yang Murray. My special thanks to Carter Wilson for the joy of being writers together. My great thanks to Vanessa Tait, too, for so much support, fun, and political wisdom; and to Craig Alderson for that invaluable boxful. Thank you to my parents for their boundless enthusiasm for my endeavors, even when they seemed dangerous.

Finally, my most profound thanks to three people whose vision, wisdom, and comradeship lie at the core of this project. With great generosity and warmth, German Zepeda welcomed me into COLSIBA and trusted me with its story. I want to thank him deeply for his friendship and for his breathtaking political wisdom; and for my first, still-inspiring trip to Nicaragua.

Thank you, Stephen Coats of US/LEAP, from the bottom of my heart for that proverbial phone call that changed my life. Stephen not only pulled me into the banana world but continues to provide a humbling example of political commitment, respect for Latin American working people, insight into true international solidarity, and steady patience in the face of seemingly overwhelming corporate power. It's been a great, if bumpy ride, Stephen.

Lastly, and most importantly, my greatest thanks go to Iris Munguía, the center of the whole story—of this book, of the women banana workers, and of my own work with them. I am still astonished at the amazing generosity with which she has invited me into her home, her family, and her work for weeks on end; and at the trust and patience with which she has shared so much with me (and also at her endless politeness, albeit with a giggle here and there, in the face of my evolving Spanish). My thanks to Ivan, Jessica, and Toño Munguía, too, for sharing the house, driving me around, helping me out, and welcoming me into the family so warmly; and to Olimpia Figueroa for welcoming me into the extended family. My own greatest hope is that this book will somehow live up to the faith that Iris placed in it, and, most importantly, serve the struggle of banana workers worldwide to build a just world for themselves and their children.

Iris Munguía (COSIBAH), Gloria García (SITRATERCO), Zoila Lagos (COSIBAH), and Domitila Hernández (SITRAESISA), near Omoa, Cortés, Honduras, returning from COSIBAH workshops in Guatemala, November 2002 (left to right).

On the Road

Of the four, Domitila Hernández, secretary of women for the Dole banana workers' union in the Aguán Valley, Honduras, came the farthest the morning of November 6, 2002. It took her four hours on a bus that left at dawn just to get to La Lima, the old United Fruit company town near San Pedro Sula in the north. Domitila was also the quietest of the four. In her early fifties, roundly built with small laughing eyes, she occupied herself on the trip weaving a pink and white plastic cover for a kleenex box. Gloria García—a bit more serious, maybe ten years younger, with tiny black braids pulled up into a knot and wearing, as usual, the snazziest outfit—got to La Lima in half an hour from her house in El Progreso. As secretary of organization for the biggest, oldest banana union in Honduras, the *Sindicato de Trabajadores de la Tela Railroad Company* (the Union of Workers of the Tela Railroad Company; SITRATERCO), she was the highest-ranking woman in the Honduran banana unions.

Iris Munguía, the political and personal force at the center of the whole story, was waiting in La Lima with the truck. In her mid forties, self-possessed, and an expert at the art of tight jeans, she had her own black braids tied back with a scarf she'd gotten in Europe from the global campaign against the World Bank. Since 1995 Iris had served as secretary of women for both the *Coordinadora de Sindicatos Bananeros y Agroindustriales de Honduras* (Coalition of Honduran Banana and Agroindustrial Unions; COSIBAH) and the *Coordinadora Latinoamericana de Sindicatos Bananeros* (Coalition of Latin American Banana Unions; COLSIBA). As it began to rain she wrapped the women's luggage, their packets of notebooks, pencils, and felt pens, and the video projector into big black plastic garbage bags and heaved them into the back of the little two-seated Nissan pickup truck.[1]

Once on the highway the three *mujeres bananeras*—banana women, as they call themselves—wove through San Pedro Sula and out of town. Passing Choloma, where the maquiladoras hulk like concentration camps—row upon row of concrete warehouses with garment and electronics factories hidden behind barbed wire— they pulled over at a bus shelter to pick up COSIBAH staffer Zoila Lagos, at fifty the jolliest, artsiest, and most politically experienced of the four. She brought the soundtrack, a cassette compiled to celebrate the tenth anniversary of the Nicaraguan Revolution. After an hour or so the women turned left at Puerto Cortés, at the coast, and headed southwest toward Guatemala, bouncing along the potholed gravel road, with Zoila and Iris belting out the songs all the way. The waters of the Caribbean lapped the coast about five hundred feet away on the right; steep green mountains loomed up to the left, as the now-afternoon light shot sideways through the palm trees. Half the bridges were out but Iris just plunged the truck right through the fords without missing a beat.

The Honduran side of the border turned out to be just a few shacks, a silent man with a stamp, and two black-market money changers. The Guatemalan side was much more serious: a bar across the road, creepier officials, and farther down the highway, a second inspection, this one by rifle-carrying, adolescent Mayan boys in camouflage fatigues. It was well after dark by the time they got to Morales and found the union hall. Selfa Sandoval, secretary of press, organization, and propaganda for the Del Monte banana workers' union in Guatemala, came rushing out to greet them, and they all ambled down to a cafe for dinner, dripping with sweat in the heat. Selfa—laughing, round, and fortyish, too, in a trim black-and-white two-piece suit she'd sewn herself—flooded the visitors with a rapid-fire report of union and personal gossip, as the male union officers dropped by to say hi.[2]

This wasn't just any union hall they'd arrived at, or just any group of union leaders. Three years earlier, in October 1999, two hundred armed paramilitaries acting in the interests of the Del

Monte Corporation had kidnapped four of the union's male leaders and twenty more of its members, held them captive in the hall, beaten them, threatened to kill them, and forced them to go on the radio to renounce their union activities. Only when each man had signed an affidavit denouncing the union did the paramilitaries allow them to leave. They fled into hiding in Guatemala City and remained underground for over two years. After a successful international campaign denouncing Del Monte, five of those men eventually went into exile in the United States; two remain in Morales as union officers. Selfa Sandoval, the only woman officer, wasn't kidnapped. But she was the one who insisted on reopening the union hall four days later, and she got her share of death threats during the next few months.[3]

At the end of the four Honduran women's journey wasn't an armed conflict, however, but something equally revolutionary: a quiet drama of transformation in the hearts and minds of women—and men—banana workers throughout Latin America. Domitila Hernández, Gloria García, Iris Munguía, and Zoila Lagos had come to town for a two-day workshop on domestic violence with twenty-three young rank-and-file women banana workers. In a seemingly quotidian journey, they were inspiring a new understanding of the gender politics of Latin American labor.

The next morning at 8:30, in the steaming hot union hall—so hot and so humid that some of the young women carried little yellow towels over one shoulder for wiping the sweat off—Selfa introduced the visitors. "We have here *compañeras de lucha* (comrades in struggle)," she began. "Here are some women you can aspire to be." Gloria García followed: "International politics are trying to divide us. We need to educate ourselves so we can confront the corporations." Zoila and Domitila, too, welcomed the participants, followed by Iris Munguía. Iris stressed the issues that women banana workers all over Latin America have in common—the hours of work, the burden of the double day. The idea, she underscored, is that we're all working together. It's not just a question of women, she said, but of gender. Men need to understand our labors, and we need to get involved in our unions. "We need to defend our organizations, and we can only do that if we know what's going on inside them." As she wrapped up her open-

ing remarks, Iris affirmed that ultimately it's about the world we
want for our kids. She called on each of the young women present
to become teachers, too, and carry the workshop's ideas back to
their packinghouses.

Glistening in their best outfits, the young women then stood
up one by one and spoke of their hopes for the workshop. "I want
to learn, and then show others." "I want to learn how to defend
myself from whoever tries to oppress me, whether it's my husband,
my union, or my boss." Last, but not least, "I want the women
from Honduras to come back five times"—although they'd just
arrived.

Zoila opened the main body of the workshop with a presentation on different definitions of domestic violence, then had the
women break up into small groups to discuss a set of quotations—
some from the Bible, some from famous men—about women's
proper place in society. Over the next two days, the women
watched a video from Mexico on domestic violence, reported back
on several group projects, played games, and cautiously entered
into guarded discussions of domestic violence, prefaced with classic phrases like "I myself haven't had any problems, but I have a
friend who…"[4]

That trip to Morales captures the core elements of the women's
projects that have quietly flourished in the banana labor movement
of Latin America since the mid 1980s. Like that road trip, the larger
story of banana women's activism starts in La Lima, Honduras, in
1985 with one union, SITRATERCO, and then expands during
the late 1990s to women activists from banana unions throughout
Honduras. It crosses borders in the late 1990s and early 2000s, not
just to Guatemala but to five other banana-exporting countries of
Central and South America as well: Colombia, Costa Rica, Ecuador,
Nicaragua, and Panamá. It's a story about how older, more experienced women banana workers are reaching out to young women
with a message of empowerment, always with an eye to the future.
Last but by no means least, it's a story of gender politics in which
men are always involved. And, as the Del Monte kidnappings un-
derscore, it's unfolding in a context of dangerous struggles with the
transnational banana corporations for which they all work. Iris's
scarf from Europe hints, moreover, at the powerful role of global

allies standing behind the banana women and their unions—just as the video from Mexico suggests women's resource networks within Latin America.

From one perspective the banana women's projects provide a straightforward example of transnational feminism, with complex roots in late twentieth-century Latin America. Their politics emerged, in part, out of women's struggles in the revolutionary movements of Central America in the 1970s and 80s—hence those songs from the Nicaraguan Revolution.[5] Many of the banana women's intellectual concepts, however, such as the distinction between sex and gender, or the idea of an *encuentro*, echo more middle-class Latin American feminisms of the 1980s and 1990s.[6] By the 1990s and 2000s the banana women's ideas, techniques, and organizing strategies also overlapped with other poor women's social movements in Latin America such as the *Mujeres por la Dignidad y la Vida* (Women for Dignity and Life; DIGNAS) in El Salvador.[7]

The banana women are distinctive from all these, though, in building women's projects within the structural form of the mixed-gender labor movement. Their transnational networks have evolved within the institutional framework of majority-male unions, at three overlapping levels: first, in individual unions; second, through national-level federations—especially COSIBAH, the Honduran banana workers' federation; and third, at the regional level, through COLSIBA, the federation of Latin American banana unions. Their local unions provide long-term institutional stability dating back to the 1950s, contracts with the banana corporations protecting union activities, and literal structures in which to organize—buildings, desks, phone lines, and, if the women can get access, computers. Their broader coalitions, in turn, provide bases for banana women to obtain and control independent funding, which they have used to launch an array of projects empowering women.[8]

These gains have come through twenty years of painstaking struggle and comradeship with individual men in the banana unions. Today, as a result, "women's work" is considered legitimate and a central part of banana unions' activities in many countries. All along, the banana women have argued that empowering women—at every level of their organizations, from the rank and file through the very top leadership—makes for stronger unions as a whole, for a more united and powerful front in the face of the corporations. They always envision their struggle as one involving men and women together, moving forward with their full powers unleashed.

Since 1985 banana workers have thus forged a powerful politics of class *and* gender, in which women's issues and union issues are inseparable and mutually reinforcing. The young banana worker at the workshop in Morales captured it exactly when she said she wanted to defend herself against anyone who wanted to push her down, whether it was her husband, her union, or her employer.

This is also a story of international labor solidarity. In the United States, two models of international solidarity dominate our imaginations: either the ugly history of intervention by the American Federation of Labor-Congress of Industrial Organizations (AFL-CIO) in Latin American labor during the Cold War; or more inspiring recent activism in support of maquiladora workers.[9] Even in the latter, though, Latin American women workers are often portrayed only as powerless, unorganized victims in need of rescue from the North.[10] The banana women show us a different tale, of powerful, savvy organizers with strong unions that fight global corporations every day and often win. They welcome aid from Europe and the United States, such as that Nissan pickup truck paid for by Catholic charities in Ireland.[11] But they're driving it, and singing their own, Latin American songs.

The banana women of Latin America offer a new model that explicitly integrates gender equity as part and parcel of any effective labor internationalism. They refuse to separate the global struggle against transnational corporations from the struggle at home for women's equality and respect. Employees of some of the biggest corporate monsters in the world with household names like Dole and Chiquita, they are also well aware that other monsters, deploying domestic violence, can inhabit their own households. They inspire us to envision a new labor internationalism that places women's issues at the center of global class politics.

Before launching into the banana world, I want to make clear my own relationship to this story. I first met the banana women when I was invited in December 2000 to help COLSIBA develop a banana union label for the US market. Since then I have worked with COLSIBA in a variety of solidarity work, mostly through the US Labor Education in the Americas Project (US/LEAP), a Chicago-based nonprofit. When I began researching the banana women I was already known to the leaders of the banana unions as an ally; I was introduced, and introduced myself, as both a researcher and someone working on behalf of the banana workers. Over the course of four years, as I interviewed three dozen male and female banana unionists and their allies, observed workshops in Guatemala, Honduras, and Nicaragua, participated in three international conferences of women banana workers, and attended four COLSIBA meetings, I was gradually embraced as part of the international network of women I was studying.

Along the way the banana women very pointedly directed and shaped my research process, teaching me both how to learn about them and what to learn. I was specifically instructed, for example, to write here that I didn't just look at documents and figures, but stayed with women banana workers in their homes, ate with them, and visited their packing plants and union offices. I, too, was along on that road trip, another round, fortyish woman belting out songs she'd learned from the Nicaraguan Revolution. Unlike the Honduran women in that truck, though, I hadn't spent twenty years packing bananas, standing up ten or twelve hours a day, six days a week. I brought all the privileges of a white, middle-class academic from the United States. But the *mujeres bananeras* of Latin America gave me another privilege: that of telling their story.

Packinghouse workers, Buenos Amigos Plantation, El Progreso, Yoro, Honduras, September 2004

CHAPTER ONE

The Work Enslaves Us

Bananas are a familiar part of the daily life of most North Americans and Europeans. But few know where their bananas come from, let alone anything about the daily life of the men and women who produce them. For over a hundred years a few giant transnationals with enormous concentrated power have controlled the Latin American banana export industry. The surprise, though, is that banana workers are often unionized—which makes all the difference for women and men banana workers alike.

First, a few broad strokes: Of all bananas produced globally, three-quarters are consumed within the country that grows them; only a quarter hit the export market. The export banana industry, in turn, is divided into two large categories. On one side are so-called ACP bananas, produced in Africa, the Caribbean, and the Philippines, representing about 19 percent of export bananas. While the big transnational corporations are increasingly producing bananas on plantations in all these regions, most ACP bananas are still grown by very small producers, usually a family unit; many are sold through a single giant conglomerate, Fyffes, based in Ireland. Fyffes, in turn, sells to a guaranteed, protected market in the European Union.[1]

Most export bananas, though, are "dollar bananas," grown in Latin America. In contrast to the ACP sphere, Latin American export bananas are overwhelmingly grown in a plantation system dating back to United Fruit's initial conquests in the 1880s. In 2004 approximately 400,000 workers labored on these banana plantations, with 150 to 300 workers on each, about one-quarter of them women.[2] Three giant transnationals with familiar names sell two-thirds of dollar bananas today: Chiquita, Dole, and Del Monte Fresh Produce, in descending order of global sales. The remainder are largely grown on plantations owned by local elites, known in the industry as "national producers." It's all about colonialism. In the ACP sphere, former European colonies sell to Europe and are in large part controlled by a European-based corporation; in the dollar sphere, countries in thrall to US-based corporations sell to US, Canadian, and European markets.

In Latin America the big three banana producers have been moving away from direct ownership of plantations since the 1950s, preferring instead to subcontract to plantations owned by the national producers, who absorb the risks and have to answer to tightly controlled quality standards—while helping the transnationals evade responsibility to their workers. The corporations still own their own docks, ships, railroads, and politicians, though, making it difficult, often impossible, for independent or small producers to reach export markets.[3]

In the past decade a new thug on the banana block has emerged, Ecuador, driving a classic global race to the bottom for banana workers. The worst culprit is Ecuador's giant Noboa Corporation, which sells Bonita brand bananas and is number five after Fyffes in global sales. By 2002 Ecuador produced 28 percent of all export bananas in the world, including one-fourth of all bananas consumed in the United States. Dole alone now gets 31 percent of its bananas from Ecuador. Since the 1970s the Ecuadoran banana industry has been entirely nonunion. Its over 250,000 workers receive as little as one-fifth the wages and benefits of banana workers elsewhere in Latin America. Their work is almost entirely casual, with no health care, vacations, retirement, or job security of any kind. That's why the banana transnationals are gradually pulling out of other parts of Latin America and sourcing from Ecuador, or using Ecuador as a pretext to lower standards elsewhere—with devastating effects throughout the region.[4]

The challenge of Ecuador has combined with a crisis in global banana overproduction since the early 1990s to put enormous pressure on the banana unions of Latin America. These unions, like the banana corporations, have a powerful history, however, and remain the core of the private-sector labor movement in Central America and Colombia. To understand them, we need to pull back a bit and look at the history of the region.

The small countries of Central America haven't been known as "banana republics" since the beginning of the twentieth century for nothing. The companies that would eventually consolidate as United Fruit and Standard Fruit (later Chiquita and Dole, respectively) moved in on Central America, Ecuador, and Colombia beginning in the 1880s and have never left, buying off, threatening, and manipulating national governments as aggressively as they originally seized the lands of peasants who resisted their incursions. In 1954 Guatemalan president Jacobo Arbenz learned the limits to any reform of the banana corporations' rule the hard way when he tried to nationalize fallow lands held by the United Fruit Company—the United States overthrew him in a coup. Throughout the twentieth century the US government backed repressive governments in the banana-producing regions to guarantee profits and "stability" for the banana corporations. Whether headed by dictators, generals, or elite oligarchs, these regimes were all held in place at the point of a US-made gun, viciously holding the lid down on workers' and peasants' protests through systematic assassinations and state terror.[5]

By the 1970s, though, the lid was flying off. In Guatemala, guerrilla movements linking urban mestizos with indigenous communities in the Highlands spread rapidly. The Guatemalan and US governments responded with two decades of horrendous repression, in which whole towns were slaughtered and buried in hidden, mass graves. In El Salvador and Nicaragua, similarly, insurgent movements rose up throughout the 1970s. At the decade's end the *Frente Sandinista de Liberación Nacional* (Sandinista National Liberation Front; FSLN), known as the *Sandinistas*, came to power in Managua. But US president Ronald Reagan, inaugurated in 1981, soon swept down in retaliation and occupied bordering Honduras for use as a military base against the Sandinistas. During the 1980s the US-funded "Contra War" killed tens of thousands of Nicaraguans and Salvadorans. The blood only stopped flowing when peace processes brokered settlements in Guatemala and El Salvador in the early 1990s, and the Sandinistas lost out to a US-sponsored slate in the 1989 elections. Repression continues today throughout the region.[6]

Most of the banana unions rose up in the 1950s and reached their greatest power just as these rebellions were emerging during the 1970s. The US-backed "counterinsurgency" project dovetailed with local elites and the banana transnationals to launch big attacks on labor throughout Latin America. First came the destruction of the Ecuadoran banana unions in the 1970s, followed by attacks on Costa Rica's labor movement, which paid a high price for solidarity with the rebellions to its west and north. In 1984 Costa Rica's banana unions counted 18,000 members, with excellent contracts and a full range of benefits. Three years later they were almost entirely wiped out by an alliance of the Costa Rican government, the Catholic Church, the US government, and the banana transnationals, which combined to introduce a bogus company union system, known as *Solidarismo*, that rapidly supplanted the legitimate unions and remains in place today on almost all corporate-allied plantations in Costa Rica.[7]

In Honduras, Guatemala, and Nicaragua, already weakened banana unions were devastated in 1998 when Hurricane Mitch wiped out plantations throughout the region. After Mitch, Chiquita, in particular, either tried to walk away from unionized plantations or replanted them with African palms (for palm oil), which require few workers. In Colombia, by contrast, banana unions have miraculously survived. They counted 17,500 members in 2004 and continue to grow, despite over two thousand assassinations of Colombian labor activists since 1991—184 killed in 2002 alone. In all these enormously hostile climates the banana unions still hang on; in 2005 they represented about 37,000 total workers in the seven countries.[8]

If we look at the big picture from the union side, we're talking Chiquita. Ninety percent of unionized banana workers work for the Cincinnati-based corporation, whose banana workers were 50 percent unionized in 2002. On all of Dole's vast directly-owned plantations, only 2,000 workers, in Honduras, have union contracts; only 1,500 Del Monte workers, in Guatemala, are unionized.[9] Starting around 1999, Chiquita executives made a decision to position their company as the "socially responsible" banana corporation. In 2001 the company signed an unprecedented agreement with COLSIBA and the International Union of Food, Agricultural, Hotel, Restaurant, Catering, Tobacco and Allied Workers' Associations (IUF), pledging to respect labor rights on its plantations and those of its subcontractors. The actual effects of the agreement are quite patchy, as Chiquita has been offloading its unionized plantations since then—most spectacularly, selling off its enormous Colombian holdings in early 2004. But the agreement has certainly held Chiquita back from overtly destroying all its unions.[10]

Whether at Chiquita, Dole, or Del Monte, unionized workers protected by contracts not only enjoy wages generally above non-union banana workers, but are protected from arbitrary firings and often receive an impressive package of benefits more important than the wage differential. Depending on the country and corporation, these benefits can include two weeks of paid vacation, paid holidays, primary education for the workers' children, health care, a modest retirement payment, and participation in their country's legally mandated social security health care system—which most nonunion employers evade.[11]

THE LIFE OF THE *MUJER BANANERA*

Women first started working on the banana plantations in the 1960s. As part of a broad restructuring prompted by containerized shipping and a new, more easily bruised variety of banana, the corporations introduced packinghouses to cut up banana stems into clumps, wash the bananas, and place them carefully into standardized 42-pound boxes. Almost all women banana workers work in the packinghouses. Except for a very few cases in Nicaragua, they are never employed in what's called the "agriculture" side of banana production—the arduous labor of tromping through the fields cutting down 75- to 120-pound stems and carrying them to cables leading to the packing plants. Nor are they ever allowed into skilled trades on the plantations, such as tractor driver, carpenter, or crop duster mechanic—all of which pay far better than work in the packing plants. In the packinghouses, by contrast, men and women work in many of the same jobs such as "deflowering" the fruit (picking off dead little flowers at each banana's end), cutting up clumps, or washing them. Other jobs are still gender specific: only women stick on brand-name labels; only men cut up the initial big stems or move boxes into shipping containers.[12]

All women banana workers' jobs are thus numbingly simple and monotonous. They stand up eight to fourteen hours a day (usually ten to twelve), for six, sometimes seven days a week, performing one of a handful of motions in a big open shed, assembly-line fashion. In the regions where bananas grow it's almost always between 95 and 105 degrees the entire year and oppressively humid. Between the sweat, the water spraying about, and the water tanks laced with fungicides, pesticides, and the latex that oozes from the cut bananas, it's dripping wet in the packinghouses. Men and women both wear rubber gloves and rubber boots the entire day.[13]

The women all say the worst part is those gloves: inside them, their hands burn with the heat. "Imagine wearing gloves all day. From 6:30 [a.m.] until 7 or 8 [p.m.] every day with gloves on," stresses Domitila Hernández.[14] That and standing up all day. Gloria García recalls that during her fourteen years in a Honduran packinghouse, her feet hurt all the time.[15] 'María Amalia,'* a rank-and-file woman banana worker from Nicaragua, describes in her autobiography how she gets up at four in the morning, travels an hour to get to work, and then stands up until six or seven at night. She's done it since she was fourteen or fifteen. "Do you know what it's like to be on your feet for thirteen hours?"[16]

A 2001 study the women unionists conducted of women banana workers in seven Latin American countries, under the auspices of COLSIBA, found a litany of other health problems caused by packinghouse work. At the top of the list were repetitive motion injuries, chemical exposure, and skin diseases caused by both the chemicals and the water. The study's respondents spoke of back injuries, premature arthritis, and cuts and falls at work. The women also reported high rates of miscarriage and rare cancers among ba-

---

*   'María Amalia' is a psuedonym, as are all the names of the women whose autobiographies appear in *Lo Que Hemos Vivido*. The authors use first names only, which I am using here in single quotations, to distinguish them from actual first names to which I refer.

nana packinghouse workers. Most of these women, without union contracts, have little or no access to health care.[17]

Working on a unionized plantation makes a huge difference for the banana women. With a union contract, women banana workers, just like the men, can usually count on a relatively permanent job for around twenty years; they can't be laid off without an extensive grievance procedure. Although contracts vary from country to country and among corporations, unionized women generally get paid vacations, pensions, holidays, and health care benefits. Unionization also provides additional benefits specific to women. In most countries where union contracts apply, there are usually no wage differences by gender for the same work. In nonunion Ecuador, by contrast, men working in packinghouses earn three or four times what the women earn for identical work. Where there are unions, sexual harassment on the job has largely been eliminated by union demand. On nonunion plantations, not only is harassment common but women are routinely fired if they become pregnant. With a union contract, women can often get maternity leave, prenatal care, and hospitalization.[18]

Daily salaries for women packinghouse workers vary dramatically from country to country, from a starvation-level low of $1 in Nicaragua to $4 in Ecuador, $6 in Honduras, $9 in Panamá, and $10 in Colombia. The most important payoff, though, isn't the salary—again, it's the benefits, which, as the corporate calculators are well aware, can amount to three or four times a given worker's salary in value. That's why it doesn't work to simply compare salaries between union and nonunion workers.[19]

With or without a union, being a *mujer bananera* doesn't end at the packinghouse. It dominates the women's every waking hour and family life. Banana work leaves very little time for anything else. One Costa Rican woman recalls, "We worked every day, sometimes from Monday through Sunday and holidays. I spent my days between two sinks of bananas, with my adolescence passing by me, leaving my youth and energy behind on that plantation."[20] As a result, the "double day" of housework and child care of the banana women is crammed into very few available hours. "Weekends don't exist for me because I use Sunday to straighten up the house," writes a Nicaraguan banana worker; she also has to cook and iron clothes for herself, her partner, and her son.[21]

The uncertain scheduling of banana production adds further stress, as the packing plants can randomly demand workers' presence for a fourteen-hour day or on Sundays with only a few hours' notice, if management suddenly wants to cut more fruit.[22] Since 1998 the corporations have deliberately instituted more "flexible" labor systems on the plantations, making the availability and hours of women's packinghouse work increasingly uncertain. "In terms of length their jobs are more and more unstable," summarizes one union report.[23]

The companies only hire young women, who generally stay for as long as they can. But very few women can bear standing on their feet for more than twenty years; so the women workers are almost all between twenty and forty, with a smattering in their forties or even fifties.[24] They're also predominantly single mothers, largely responsible for their own housework—in contrast to male banana workers, who can count on female companions or mothers for cooking, cleaning, and child-care services. The women's study, discussing the predominance of single mothers, concluded: "The general opinion was that a great deal of paternal irresponsibility persists, and that men frequently abandon their responsibilities to their children and female partners."[25] The combination of single parenthood, long distances from home to workplace, and long hours of wage work, combined with housework, is brutal. 'Carmen,' a banana union leader from Honduras who raised two kids on her own, sums up:

> The work on the banana plantations enslaves us, because we work twelve hours a day or longer; that means that we almost don't live with our families and our children are looked after by our siblings, aunts and uncles, or grandparents, those of us that have family support; those who don't, their children are left alone. Most of the women are both father and mother to their kids.[26]

Domitila Hernández and Iris Munguía both volunteered the same common saying: "They say that on the banana plantations, we don't raise our children—our families do."[27]

Historically, most banana workers in Latin America have lived on company-owned housing clustered near or on one edge of the plantation. Classic company houses are wooden, either a two-family unit with a room downstairs for each family to cook and eat in, another upstairs for sleeping, and perhaps an open space for hanging hammocks; or a long row on the same model. More recent company-owned houses are made of cinder block. They have a gloomier feel, but as one banana woman explained, "A *bloque* is better than the wooden houses because it's easier to clean, and doesn't fall over in a storm"—no small consideration in hurricane country.[28] In recent years the corporations have begun selling off company houses to the workers, in a long-term move away from paternalism, but the alternatives can be even worse—and certainly more expensive. In all cases, substandard housing makes housework even more difficult.[29]

Wherever the women live, banana cultivation permeates their lives, literally. Although the companies are legally barred from spraying where people are present, and the situation has improved dramatically in recent years, the women still live daily lives not far from the aerial crop spraying of pesticides.[30] The unions' survey of banana women concludes with this chillingly eloquent passage:

> The women in the banana zones often face the effects that banana production has on the environment: when they wash clothes, when they cook food, when they want to keep a garden or cultivate a small plot in areas near the plantation, in their reproductive lives when they or their partners are contaminated with agrochemicals that produce birth defects or malfunctions in their bodies.[31]

In all the countries, moreover, water quality is usually terrible, often poisoned by chemical spills from the same companies.[32]

If banana packinghouse work is dangerous, exhausting, and, in the women's own words, "enslaving," the banana regions' lack of economic development leaves the women with few other options for employment. The only other jobs lie in the informal economy—usually making and selling food in small batches or sometimes working as a domestic servant. Most women banana workers have only a sixth-grade education—in Guatemala, the worst case, 34 percent are illiterate—which further limits their choices. With steady employment at a living wage, unionized or not, women banana workers are in fact the lucky ones. Until they're forty. After that, it's grim. Age combined with gender discrimination leaves only the informal economy or family networks to help them survive. When they leave the packinghouse, women from unionized plantations receive, though, a lump-sum pension payment of perhaps $2,000, which they use to help buy a house, start a tiny business, or pay a *coyote* to get them into the United States to be with children who are increasingly forced to migrate.[33]

Why are so few other choices available? Since the debt crises of the 1980s, neoliberal economic policies imposed by the United States through the International Monetary Fund (IMF) and World Bank have tightened the noose around all these Latin American countries. As part of structural adjustment programs to pay back loans, their governments have been forced to conform to a tight formula: cut back State-funded social services, privatize government-owned entities, and reduce the economy to two export tracks, instituted through new free trade agreements—export agriculture in open and disastrous competition with more powerful economies in the North, and maquiladora-style industrial development. The results have been disastrous throughout Latin America. And there's no place at all in this model for women over twenty-five; no jobs, no safety net.[34]

The banana women's situation, in other words, is always precarious. Trapped in the cold arms of the banana transnationals, the women's fate is intertwined not only with the global banana industry, but also with the future of the banana labor movement. And they know it. That's why, beginning in the mid 1980s, they fought so hard for a place within it.

Packinghouse worker, Buenos Amigos Plantation, El Progreso, Yoro, Honduras, September 2004

Mirian Reyes, pioneer of SITRATERCO women's work, August 2003

CHAPTER TWO

SITRATERCO

Women's Power Is Union Power

Right off the *Plaza Central* in the middle of La Lima, Honduras, across from the *Banco de Los Trabajadores*, there's a pistachio green, two-story union hall with SITRATERCO in big black letters marching across its front, over the door, for the *Sindicato de Trabajadores de la Tela Railroad Company* (Union of Workers of the Tela Railroad Company). In late 2002, if you walked in that door, after your eyes adjusted from the glaring sun outside you would see in the front hall a pink-and-white display with headlines like "The Practice of Citizenship," "Women Have Rights," and "Public Participation" kept over from a conference of women banana workers earlier that year. Follow the wide stairs up to the second floor into the big meeting hall, and you would see an eight-foot wide banner reading "*BIENVENID@S COMPANER@S A OTRO AÑO DE LUCHA INCLAUDIBLE POR LA DEFENSA DE LOS DERECHOS DE L@S TRABAJADORE/AS*" (WELCOME COMRADES TO ANOTHER YEAR OF UNCEASING STRUGGLE FOR THE DEFENSE OF WORKERS' RIGHTS). In Spanish, the word *trabajadores* has been altered so that an "a" fits inside the "e." Similarly, *compañeros* has an "a" inside the "o" at the end. Sexist language, in other words, has been purged from the union's public presence—just one clue, along with the exhibit in the hall, that something special has happened in the gender politics of this union.[1]

The story of women banana workers' empowerment and the transformation of their unions begins slowly in the mid 1980s on the north coast of Honduras, deep inside that union with the pistachio green building, SITRATERCO. This is where the first, biggest, and most painful battles to establish women's programs for banana workers were fought during the 1980s and 90s. This is where the women first successfully gained union leadership, and where they first transformed themselves—and their menfolk—so dramatically.

SITRATERCO itself was born in a mass strike from May through July 1954 from which all Honduran labor history flows. That spring, 25,000 workers at the Tela Railroad Company, a United Fruit Company subsidiary; 11,000 at its rival, Standard Fruit; and several thousand Honduran workers from other sectors all walked out at once, producing a huge national crisis. The US embassy moved quickly to try to control the situation, working hand-in-glove with the AFL-CIO and the Honduran government to identify and repress alleged Communist leaders, on the one hand, and to promote its own carefully selected anti-Communist leaders, on the other. Workers at Standard Fruit settled their strike with only minor gains after two weeks. But at United Fruit, the strikers held out for ten weeks. As the situation threatened higher and higher levels of chaos for the Honduran government and fruit companies, strike committee leaders not to the US embassy's liking were systematically arrested, until the final group bore no relation to those who had originally launched the strike. By the time the strike committee finally signed a US-brokered settlement, sixty-nine days after the strike commenced, United Fruit had agreed to grant minor pay increases and scattered benefits, and the AFL-CIO had wormed its way into control of the big new banana union that emerged by summer's end, SITRATERCO.

A powerful Cold War compromise ensued that would stay in place for twenty years. The arrangement—horse-traded during the mid 1950s between the Honduran government, the banana corporations, the US State Department, and the AFL-CIO—neatly cut rank-and-file Honduran banana workers out of the loop. The companies, fearful of Communism and under State Department pressure, agreed to recognize the unions, and eventually, after repeated strikes, granted lucrative contracts guaranteeing job security, health care, holidays, vacations, and modest pensions. In exchange they got captive, US-controlled unions that shut Leftists out of union leadership, stayed out of electoral politics, and never attacked the US corporate presence in the country. And, of course, they never got a Communist revolution.[2]

Throughout the late 1950s, 60s, and 70s the AFL-CIO groomed and controlled SITRATERCO's leadership through the American Institute for Free Labor Development (AIFLD) and the *Organización Regional Interamericana de Trabajadores* (Interamerican Regional Federation of Workers; ORIT). With millions in US State Department money, the AFL-CIO bought houses for union leaders; it paid salaries; it funded regular trips to a special cushy anti-Communist training center in Virginia. Rank-and-file members, for their part, got subsidized housing and food cooperatives. Under this model SITRATERCO's membership, 25,000 at its inception, stabilized by the mid 1970s at 10,000. It was the jewel in the crown of the Honduran labor movement, the most powerful private sector union in Central America, and the model for AFL-CIO fantasies of controlling the entire Latin American labor movement.[3]

The AFL-CIO's Cold War legacy in the long run also, ironically, helped opened the space for women banana workers' later activism to develop. First, it funded SITRATERCO's 1960 two-story building in La Lima and eventually a union schoolhouse three blocks away. Second, the AFL-CIO's agents negotiated contracts with United Fruit and Standard Fruit that provided an average of two weeks of paid time off for rank-and-file union members to attend union education workshops—originally, to ensure their ideological adherence to anticommunism, as well as to train banana workers in US-style collective bargaining and grievance procedures. In the 1980s and 90s women banana unionists would use both union halls and that time off for their own version of union education.[4]

Moreover, in part because the AFL-CIO was busily claiming to support "free and democratic" trade unions in contrast to "totalitarian" Communism, SITRATERCO's internal structure guaranteed a serious measure of internal democracy. In contrast to US unions, usually controlled by permanent, paid, often middle-class staff members, SITRATERCO's by-laws create an executive committee of six officers—president, secretary-general, finance secretary, secretary of organization, grievance secretary, and recording secretary, in roughly descending order of status and power—all directly elected by the members at conventions. They all receive a salary paid for by members' dues assessments. And they have all, historically, been actual banana workers. When they end their mandatory four-year terms, they go right back to their old jobs on the plantations.[5]

When women first entered United Fruit packinghouses represented by SITRATERCO in the early 60s, they were entirely shut out of the upper reaches of the union. During the 1960s and early 70s, a few women were marginally involved in the union as individuals, but they held no offices and had no power. Then, in 1975, Left-affiliated men took control of SITRATERCO's leadership. AFL-CIO loyalists threw them out within two years, but during that period the men on the Left were able to introduce, for reasons unrelated to gender politics, a further level of democracy to SITRATERCO's structure. This, too, would later mean everything for the women. Each plantation now had its own, elected *comité de la base*, or rank-and-file committee, replicating the same set of officers as the executive committee—only without a president. They also created two new subsections between the base committees and the executive committee, each with two of its own officers who worked part-time for the union and part-time on the plantation. Plantation-level officers got time off for some meetings but otherwise labored in their original jobs.[6]

By the late 70s a handful of individual women had been elected to these base committees, and it was tough. 'Emilia,' who joined SITRATERCO in 1974, recalls that in her sector, Higuerito, "the secretary general was a woman; she was dealing with the politics all alone and that inspired me to help support her because sometimes the guys humiliated her because she was a woman."[7] It's unclear who this woman officer was, or how she got elected, but for any woman running for office, numbers were everything. On any given plantation, because only men worked in the fields, they always outnumbered women three or four to one. But a further structural change in the late seventies finally opened the door for women to fully enter the union—although again, that was not its intention. This time SITRATERCO split the base committees into two separate, autonomous committees: one for the agricultural division, all

male, and one for the packinghouse, about 80 percent female. By
the early 80s women could finally elect other women into office
for their plantation base committee, usually as *secretaria de actas*
(recording secretary), the bottom rung.[8]

Then, in 1984–85, women members of SITRATERCO start-
ed for the first time to strategize together across plantations and,
equally important, to understand themselves collectively as women.
"The rank-and-file women started to consolidate as a group and
struggle in new ways," recalls 'Luisa,' a SITRATERCO activist of
this generation.[9] In part, it was the women's new potential ability
to get elected. They also got very angry, and then motivated, when
the male leadership suddenly appropriated all of an educational
grant from the International Labor Organization (ILO), to which
the women had thought they'd have access.[10]

The winds of Central American Left feminism were blowing
across the border into Honduras in these years too, as women
revolutionary militants in Nicaragua, El Salvador, and Guatemala
discovered that even if they could carry a rifle, that didn't mean
their male comrades would let them share power. The Sandinistas'
1979 triumph in Nicaragua especially underscored this contradic-
tion.[11] Women militants "felt very bad about the revolutionary
movement" when they found themselves shut out after the victory, Norma Iris Rodríguez, a Honduran campesina activist recalls.
She remembers nascent women's groups in the Honduran peasant movement during the mid 1980s as well, that filtered over
into SITRATERCO women's awareness. SITRATERCO, though,
Rodríguez underscores, was the first place where women's issues
emerged in the Honduran labor movement.[12]

In 1986 women members of SITRATERCO launched their
first and most important campaign in the union, and the proverbial excrement hit the fan. At the union's biannual congress Gladys
Valle and María Teresa Aguilar introduced a motion asking the
union to create a separate *Comité Femenino* (Women's Committee)
with official status and its own officers selected by the committee.
Every account of this part of the story repeats the same phrase:
"The men thought they were crazy."[13] Worse, another woman
recalls, "Some of the male comrades were laughing at us."[14] The
measure was completely defeated. But opposition only motivated

the women to work harder. "Disappointed and feeling really put down, I felt awful when I saw that male comrades that represented the rank-and-file women didn't approve the motion," recalls 'Luisa.'[15]

The women then developed what one woman called "a subtle political approach."[16] Over the next two years they identified, one by one, individual sympathetic men officers and won them slowly over to support the *acta* establishing the Women's Committee.[17] During the same period, "when we went out on strike the women's participation was really clear and the men comrades started to be more aware of how powerful the women were in their support for the union's struggle; they saw that women were crucial; we weren't afraid to confront the different problems that came up."[18] In 1988 the women again introduced their proposal at the SITRATERCO congress, and this time it passed—with eight women and 120 men voting. At the last minute their opponents tried to rescind it, but the women threatened to ally themselves with the union's far right, and the measure passed.[19]

TRANSFORMATION

"After the *acta*, everything changed," remembers Gloria García.[20] The women had not only won men over to the need for women's empowerment, but they now had their own official independent structure for activities within the union, ushering in the first flowering of the *Comité Femenino* from 1989 through 1993. In 1988 the activists organized their first general assembly of SITRATERCO women and elected their first committee and its president; they then created subcommittees on all the plantations, around twenty-five at the time. They also painstakingly wrote their own grant proposal to the ILO for women's work in SITRATERCO.[21]

One particularly important project focused the deep excitement of these early years, while establishing future patterns for the women's work. In 1990 Iris Munguía and Norma Murillo attended a series of workshops in Costa Rica sponsored by the ILO and the Danish labor movement on "Women, Work, and Unions in the Agricultural Sector of Developing Nations." Every three months, for two years, Iris and Norma traveled to Costa

Rica, where they studied for two weeks. When they came home after each class, Iris and Norma, in turn, trained the eleven other members of SITRATERCO's Women's Committee in what they'd just learned. They passed around twenty-six little booklets they had brought back from Costa Rica, from a series entitled The Role of Rural Women Workers in Society, with themes like *Talking about Difference*, *Woman and Society*, and *Woman and Work*.[22] The women from the *Comité Femenino*, in turn, promised to each train twenty-five additional women at the plantation level.

It was a grand scheme of collective education and empowerment sustained with very few resources. The whole thing happened on Sundays, after work, for four years. "The work wasn't easy because it was the only day that the women comrades had to be with their children and clean their houses," recalls 'Carmen,' one of the original group. "So I visited them in their homes, to raise their consciousness and inspire them to attend the workshops for the three hours that they usually went on in the afternoon."[23] But the enthusiasm was enormous. "The fact that some of the women didn't know how to read or write didn't keep them from participating."[24]

Through this early project the women refined their core educational method, the workshop, a form they learned in part from the ILO workshop in Costa Rica, but more directly from middle-class Leftist men, often academics, who had helped them out in their earlier years, such as Mario Posas or German Leizelar (currently minister of labor in Honduras).[25] From three hours to two days long, a given workshop drew together ten or twenty women for fun, comradeship, and education. Their first workshop was called "A Profile of Leadership," which the women chose because they wanted to "get women involved as officers at the plantation level."[26] Other first-round topics similarly focused on women's empowerment within the union in relation to both their male comrades and corporate management—grievance procedures, for example, or parliamentary procedures. Through these discussions, and with input from the ILO materials, they gradually started addressing gender issues more directly. "Through the educational process 'Gender Issues' developed," one woman recalls.[27] A new round of workshops added new titles like "Sex and Gender."[28]

Without question, through the combination of workshops and union struggles, this generation of women deeply transformed themselves. In part it was the experience of holding union office. 'Luisa,' who served first as recording secretary, then grievance secretary for her packinghouse committee, underscores: "Taking on a position like that, with so much responsibility, meant a really powerful change of character."[29] Iris Munguía, who similarly began as recording secretary in 1982, recalls, "The best school was to be a *dirigenta de la base* [rank-and-file level officer]."[30] She memorized key passages of both the union's contract with Chiquita and the Honduran Labor Code. At the same time these original leaders were learning to lead workshops for other women, while inventing how to talk about touchy issues of sex and gender. Mirian Reyes, who would eventually go on to direct educational projects for a nationwide labor federation, remembers, "At first I was really scared to discuss sex and gender and the sexual division of labor." But as she moved around from plantation to plantation, leading the same workshop, she grew less and less fearful.[31]

These first leaders were very conscious of their own position as role models to other women banana workers in the union, and of the other women's support for their self-development. "They supported us in educating ourselves so that we could serve as models for other women using consciousness-raising," writes 'Emilia.'[32] 'Luisa' speaks of the women's goals:

> We knew that the women comrades that we brought to the workshops supported us just by being there in all our struggles, but we needed them to be more forceful, to express what they were feeling, to stop being submissive; because most of them kept silent. We felt satisfied in the end because by the time they left they were very active and articulate women, who through education were improving.[33]

In telling their own stories, these same SITRATERCO women leaders in turn repeatedly name other individual women who encouraged them to attend a workshop, speak up, or run for office.[34]

For all their glorious self-transformation, though, the women pioneers all remained deeply embattled during these years. On the one hand, they had to fight tooth and nail with men within

SITRATERCO. "We were struggling to maintain the Women's Committee and at the same time battling the male comrades' machismo, because they were opposed to women managing the funds the ILO sent."[35] Undaunted, the women pressed on with further proposals. "Who cared what pissed off the guys?" recalls 'Luisa.'[36] They constantly felt they had to prove to the men—as well as to themselves and to other women—that they could do the actual work of union officers. "My biggest experience was trying to convince the macho comrades that we women *could* do it when we wanted to," recalls Gloria García, one of the first two women to serve as an officer at the section level.[37]

On another front Chiquita was also taking notice of how this new female activism was strengthening SITRATERCO's rank-and-file base and increasing its willingness to act militantly. During these same years, the late 1980s, Left leaders finally wrested control of the union's top offices. On a broader stage, revolutionary movements continued to contest power in Guatemala and El Salvador, and even ruled in Nicaragua until 1989. In 1997, Chiquita tried to introduce a company-union system, replicating *Solidarismo*, which had successfully wiped out the Costa Rican banana unions in the mid and late 80s.[38] In an effort to split up the union's female activists, women in particular were targeted for corporate-welfare schemes. At the same time the company came down especially hard on women militants during strikes. Throughout these years, "we always thought we'd get fired" for high levels of union activism, the women recall.[39]

'Carmen' serves as a good example of what these women went through. She first attended a *Comité Femenino* workshop in 1990, when she was thirty-one. The next year she attended SITRATERCO's second *Asamblea de Mujeres* (Women's Assembly), where she was elected as a member of the committee for the next two years. Then, in 1992, her fellow packinghouse workers elected her grievance secretary for Naranjo Chino Plantation (that year four women were elected to its committee, and only one man, as recording secretary, the token job usually granted to a woman). Two years later she moved up even further, when they elected her secretary general of her plantation. That was when things got nasty. The finance secretary of her plantation claimed that her election wasn't valid because the lights went out during the meeting. But German Zepeda, then secretary of organization on SITRATERCO's top-level executive committee, overrode him. Then, in 1995, 'Carmen' was elected grievance secretary for her entire section, El Progreso, and it got worse. "My work comrade, the secretary general of the El Progreso Section, was *machista* and started trying to make it look like I was doing a bad job."[40]

For many women of this generation, who founded the *Comité Femenil* while simultaneously pioneering as women in union office, the challenge of sustaining both activities while working in the packinghouses was overwhelming. 'Luisa' recalls: "Working at the rank-and-file level, I spent more time dealing with the problems of the male comrades. They felt isolated and forgotten, and that depressed me, but I couldn't leave the leadership of the Women's Committee because I was the one that had proposed it in the first place and then had fought for it in the union."[41]

At every turn, they framed their struggle for *women's* equality and empowerment in terms of *union* power. SITRATERCO, they argued, could only take on Chiquita if it fully unleashed women's as well as men's militance. They did not cast women's work in individualistic terms of personal liberation or self-expression; rather, they presented themselves in collective terms, as comrades in struggle who were prevented from fully participating by sexism.

"1994 was a year of big victories for the women," remembers 'Emilia.'[42] In early January sixty women came together in La Lima for an unprecedented three-day workshop on gender issues and leadership development. 'Carmen,' who "had the privilege of leading that workshop," writes that for her "it was a complete success, seeing so many women who wanted to learn more and who wanted to participate more actively in our union."[43] That year women also played prominent roles in supporting major strikes. They also elected their fourth woman, Iris Munguía, to the executive committee of SITRATERCO—though still no more than one woman had served at any given moment.[44]

Four years later women had further consolidated their power at the union's top. The Women's Committee was thriving; "We had a really tight organization, we were really united, there was a lot of work and responsibility."[45] At the union's 1998 general congress, more women participated than ever before in the 44-year history of SITRATERCO, and Gloria García was elected secretary general at the section level.[46]

SURVIVAL AND SOLIDARITY

Then, on October 26, 1998, Hurricane Mitch hit, and the whole world changed. Mitch was one of the largest hurricanes of the twentieth century. In the last week of October 1998 and the first week of November, it tore through Guatemala, Honduras, and Nicaragua, then back through Honduras to the Caribbean, killing more than nine thousand people, 5,657 in Honduras alone. Ten percent of the country's entire population lost their homes. Mitch was particularly devastating to the banana plantations of Honduras' north coast, where it destroyed 87 percent of the country's 1999 banana crop and 100 percent of Chiquita's. SITRATERCO, and its women in particular, faced the immediate task of feeding thousands of workers whose homes had been inundated with mud, as well as the longer-term economic fact that most of the plantations at which they worked were shut down, possibly for good. Even on those plantations that Chiquita chose to replant the next year, women would be hit hardest, since it took nine months for banana plants to produce fruit for the packinghouses.[47]

But many plantations never did reopen. Chiquita used Mitch to accelerate the process of pulling out of direct banana production that had been underway for more than a decade. It was selling its plantations to independent, national producers, then turning around and buying fruit from them—to avoid risk and labor costs. As a result SITRATERCO's membership, which had been plummeting long before Mitch, dropping from 10,000 in 1990 to 6,000 right before the hurricane, shrank even further to 4,850 after Mitch. Chiquita, to avoid labor costs and union power, just left fields fallow, or replanted them with African palm-oil palms, which require few workers. Most recently it has cut back on the labor needs of its directly-owned banana plantations by installing a new, more efficient system of dual-row planting and overhead cables.[48]

By 2003 SITRATERCO was a shadow of its former self. It still had its two buildings, its buses, its commissary, and, most important of all, the militance and pride of its members and its tradition of democratic self-management and union education. But Chiquita's stratagems to reduce its unionized workforce on directly-owned plantations had taken a severe toll. SITRATERCO still had the power to enforce its contracts and protect its members' job security and benefits packages. But it only had 2,100 members.[49]

Of that 2,100, eight hundred women remained. "We note with great concern that the membership in our organization has diminished considerably," mourned the *Comité Femenino* in its 2002 report. "We were not prepared to deal with this situation, because of which, many of our comrades have been obliged to ask for their *prestaciones* [lump-sum pension payments paid out when workers permanently leave employment] since the closure of some plantations by the banana transnationals." They noted the ensuing grave prospects for women over thirty who "are not accepted in the labor market."[50]

In reiterating the committee's objectives in the face of this situation, SITRATERCO's Women's Committee nonetheless affirmed the ongoing spirit of women's work in the union, their mixed-gender approach to education, and their highest goals:

•To strengthen the organizational capacity of women's work in the union, workplace, and social fronts, and by doing so strengthen our union in its current struggle.

•To implement educational programs with mixed-gender participation.

•To struggle for the full integration of women at the national level.

•To struggle for gender equity.[51]

Asked in 2002 about the current situation of women in SITRATERCO, Gloria García noted a decline of women's activism at the lower level. In 2000, nine of SITRATERCO's base committees had female general secretaries; in 2002, only five. She felt that women were getting weaker, less interested in activism.[52] But at the upper level, both she and Iris Munguía stressed, women were more powerful than ever, with two of six positions on the executive committee and one of four middle-level officers.[53] Today, no one in SITRATERCO would think to challenge the institutionalized power of the *Comité Femenino* or female officers.

On August 28, 2004, SITRATERCO celebrated its fiftieth anniversary with a big ceremony, a soccer game (against visiting banana unionists from Guatemala), a marimba band, and later that night, a free dance in the union hall. During the ceremony, after the mass and before the honoring of retirees, two presentations outlined key moments in the union's history, in up-to-date Power Point. The first, by Nelson Nuñez, celebrated the 1954 general strike in which the union was born. In the second, Iris Munguía highlighted *"Luchas y Logros de las Mujeres Sindicalistas Bananeras"* (Struggles and Achievements of Women Banana Unionists). At SITRATERCO's most important public event in a long time, in other words, the union recognized women members' projects to be just as central to the union's identity and history as its triumphant founding.[54]

Iris began her talk by naming individual heroic women during the general strike, then named more and more outstanding women pioneers, including the founders of the *Comité Femenino*. She didn't shirk from naming the health hazards, long hours, and triple days still facing banana women—or the "machismo and distrust on the part of their life partners." But she also noted that women's participation in the unions had grown enormously, and she celebrated the changes wrought by years and years of work involving both men and women. At the very end of her presentation, though, Iris couldn't resist spontaneously asking the assembled crowd how it had been possible, in fifty years, that SITRATERCO had never had even one woman president.[55]

SITRATERCO still awaits its first woman president or secretary general, but there's no question that the union has utterly transformed itself since its women members first started talking together in the mid 1980s. A November 2002, photograph of six upper-level SITRATERCO officers in front of the union's office in La Lima, on their way back from contract negotiations with Chiquita executives, captures the depth of comradeship, equality, and ease between men and women in the union. The officers are all laughing, standing close together; two men in short-sleeved dress shirts each hang an arm casually over the shoulders of Sergia Marina Cárdenas, grievance secretary for the El Progreso section, in a white SITRATERCO T-shirt and a khaki green skirt. Elba Martínez, recording secretary, standing close in with the group, is laughing too.[56] Above all, it's the sheer ease of these women's position alongside their enthusiastic menfolk that sums up women's accomplishments in SITRATERCO. The union knows it's in deep, deep trouble. But it also knows that it is more powerful in addressing its troubles because the women and men stand together, and the powers of both in fighting for the union are unleashed.

Members of SITRATERCO negotiating committee returning from meeting with Chiquita, La Lima, Cortés, Honduras, November 2002

COSIBAH staff, La Lima, Cortés, Honduras, November 2002;
Belkis Castro, Iris Munguía, Nelson Nuñez, Zoila Lagos, Angela
Aranda, German Zepeda, Roberto Morales (left to right).

CHAPTER THREE

Honduras
A Free Space

On August 22, 2003, six young maquiladora workers—three men, three women—crowded into a back office in the La Lima headquarters of the *Coordinadora de Sindicatos Bananeros y Agroindustriales de Honduras* (Coalition of Honduran Banana and Agroindustrial Unions; COSIBAH). They wanted to organize a union and had come to Nelson Nuñez, a COSIBAH organizer, because they'd heard he could help them. Nelson carefully explained the legal process involved—and the risks. Chances were all six would be fired the minute they filed a legal petition with their names on it. He chatted with them for an hour or so. Just before they left, he casually handed to each of the visitors a pamphlet produced by women banana unionists earlier that year, entitled *Conozcamos de Género* (Learning About Gender). "Learning Together," its cover celebrated. Inside, it discussed themes such as "The Sexual Division of Labor," "Gender Identity," and "What Is Sex and What Is Gender?" The back cover listed "Some Obstacles to Women's Participation in Organizations." The sheer normalcy of this moment is breathtaking: a militant, dedicated union *man* signaling to young workers, both men and women, that gender equality is, of course, a central part of union work.[1]

As the scene suggests, the story of women banana workers doesn't end with SITRATERCO. Starting in 1994 Honduran banana women expanded their activism into COSIBAH, a new nationwide body. COSIBAH was the reward for the women's hard-fought, painful battles in SITRATERCO. It gave them a new institutional space in which to spread the SITRATERCO model throughout the banana labor movement of Honduras during the late 1990s and 2000s, mainstreaming and legitimating banana women's projects. At the same time COSIBAH gave women activists much more independence—including, eventually, their own funding—than they had ever had in SITRATERCO. As the presence of those six maquiladora workers in the federation's office indicates, moreover, COSIBAH also made possible links between women banana workers and poor Honduran women in other economic sectors. Finally—and here it gets even more interesting—COSIBAH also drew supportive men much more deeply into women's work.

COSIBAH grew out of a crisis in the global banana industry that long predated Hurricane Mitch. After the collapse of the Soviet Union in 1989, the big banana transnationals thought, wrongly, that huge markets were going to open up in Russia and Eastern Europe, and expanded their plantings throughout the world. When the new markets never materialized, global banana prices plummeted in 1991 and 1992 in a grand crisis of overproduction. To recoup their profits, the corporations turned nasty on their unions, seeking to squeeze higher profits out of each plantation. These were the years they began to threaten to go to Ecuador if unions didn't grant contract concessions.[2]

In response, in 1994 key figures in SITRATERCO brought together seven banana unions spread widely across the valleys of the north coast of Honduras to form COSIBAH, a national coalition based in La Lima. Altogether its affiliates represented 12,000 workers at Dole and Chiquita.[3] COSIBAH soon launched joint educational activities for all the banana unions and began to coordinate bargaining with both corporations at a national level, while emerging as the public face of the Honduran banana workers. Much of the energy behind COSIBAH came from banana workers on the Left, as Honduran activists emerged from the nightmare of the US Contra War against the Sandinistas, finally sloughed off AFL-CIO domination, and sought to express *una nueva visión sindical* (a new union vision) to use the title of COSIBAH's newsletter.[4]

For all the impressive achievements of women in SITRATERCO, at the point of COSIBAH's founding women's work in the other six banana unions was nonexistent. Outside of SITRATERCO, not a single woman held office, even at the plantation level; they had no separate committee structures for the packing plants or special positions or committees for women at any level. In SITRATERCO, by contrast, women were just then achieving their greatest victories. The SITRATERCO leaders who founded COSIBAH included key women activists and some of their closest male allies. Together, they deliberately created the position of secretary of women as the second most important office in the new federation. In doing so they established the institutional legitimacy of women's work in COSIBAH and, implicitly, throughout its affiliates. Equally important, they created the organizational platform for women's independent funding and activism.[5]

It's impossible to separate the story of COSIBAH's secretary of women from the woman who has held the position since it was created. Iris Munguía was born in 1957 into a banana worker family and grew up in company housing on Finca Indiana, near La Lima. She finished the sixth grade, then worked as a seamstress and in the informal economy. In 1975, when she was eighteen, she started working in a packinghouse. She figured she'd work there for about five years, then do something else. But she got pregnant and had her first kid at twenty, and soon had two more children with her banana-worker husband. She felt then she was trapped. As she stood in the line, cutting, packing, cutting, packing, she began to dream of her children's futures, not her own. She belonged to SITRATERCO but wasn't involved in it.[6]

But then, in 1989, a coworker pulled her into SITRATERCO activism and she jumped into women's work in the glory years of the *Comité Femenino*. She started out as an educator, then a plantation-level officer, and quickly emerged as a pioneering woman activist. Iris was one of the two original women who traveled to Costa Rica for three years to train as an educator on women's issues. In these same years she returned to school, taking classes at night, and worked her way up to the community-college level. Meanwhile, in SITRATERCO, Iris became the third woman to serve as a secretary general of a base committee, the first to serve as an officer at the section level, and the fourth woman to reach the union's executive committee. When she was offered COSIBAH's new position as secretary of women, she accepted it eagerly.[7]

Like all of the COSIBAH staff, Iris is a tremendously hard worker. She's also a great listener, constantly learning, borrowing ideas, and educating herself. She has high status in the banana unions in part because when she leads, it's never about *her*, it's about her desire to celebrate and advance all the banana workers. The depth of her faith in the other women—and her male comrades—in many ways holds the whole enterprise of COSIBAH women's work together. Iris is also a very careful strategist who never thinks or acts without having her ducks lined up. All in all, she has the quiet, dignified power that comes with the deep respect of her peers. Which doesn't mean she lacks a sense of humor, combined with healthy self-esteem. Picture one 2003 COSIBAH meeting with a representative from each of its affiliates—maybe six men, two women—already in the room. Iris strolled in wearing giant pink curlers and a Day-Glo orange scarf tied artfully over the whole of it, and didn't even blink.[8]

In 1995, with Iris newly established in the COSIBAH office, SITRATERCO's activist women carefully launched a national program under the new federation's rubric. They started with research. First they created teams based on SITRATERCO's *Comité Femenil* and paid official visits to the officers of all the unions. Then they visited every unionized banana plantation in the country. At each one they organized a women's workshop on the theme "Talking About Difference" and organized a Women's Committee to investigate issues confronting women banana workers. Along the way they distributed pamphlets, notebooks, and other materials they'd accumulated in their own work over the years.[9]

When each new *Comité Femenil* produced its findings, the women compiled all the information into a single report, stressing four themes: first, women banana workers' labor conditions (long, irregular work days, gender discrimination in salaries, union repression, contract violations); second, occupational health and safety (from agrochemicals to reproductive rights); third, education (including access to union education); and fourth, women's status in the unions (their absence from leadership and the lack of recognition of Women's Committees or secretaries of women).[10]

Next, in 1996 they organized the First National Conference of Banana Women in San Pedro Sula. The conference reveals how carefully the women strategized and how cleverly they enlisted powerful men to endorse women's demands—or at least neutralized their potential opposition. Under the official auspices of COSIBAH, they gathered not only a total of sixty-five women from all the banana union affiliates, but also their male officers, plus leaders and representatives from regional and national Honduran labor federations, the banana unions of Nicaragua and Costa Rica, the International Union of Food Workers, the Danish labor movement, national women's groups, and the press. They asked German Zepeda, president of COSIBAH, and Ajax Irías, a Left trade-union activist, to give opening speeches, followed with one by Iris Munguía.[11]

After an official presentation of the women's research report, conference participants broke into teams, many of them mixed-gender, to discuss themes echoing its findings. Those teams, in turn, produced a series of official agreements on which all the officers present—including the male leaders of the affiliates—signed off. The agreements give a good glimpse into the exact ways in which COSIBAH framed women's issues at its outset. First, health and safety: they asked each union's executive committee to demand that the companies provide better protective equipment and more training on reproductive health. Second, education: the unions should stimulate the participation of women in formal education—including provision of transportation—and include women in union education programs. Moreover, the theme of gender should be integrated into union education and "directed as much to men as to women." A third agreement addressed women's status in the unions: bylaws should be changed to give legal recognition to the secretary of women and women's demands should be integrated into contracts with the corporations. Fourth, the unions should demand complete compliance with the contracts and unite all seven unions to confront the banana corporations regarding women's labor conditions. Fifth, and finally, the conference agreements exhorted COSIBAH to establish relationships with other women's groups in Honduras and with women in other labor sectors, especially the maquiladoras, domestic workers, campesinas, health care workers, and teachers. All in all, in the sweep of these demands, in the breadth of participation, and in the enlistment of both men's and women's endorsement, the San Pedro Sula conference was a big moment in Honduran labor history, full of energy, excitement, and hopes.[12]

Of course, signing agreements didn't change the other unions overnight. But because the agreements came through COSIBAH, with so many of the male big shots from the unions present, the conference legitimated women's work bridging *all* the Honduran banana unions, not just SITRATERCO.

COSIBAH created the space for the SITRATERCO women to extend their education-and-leadership development model to hundreds of other banana workers. Between 1995 and 1998 COSIBAH sponsored six to eight workshops a year for women and men in all the affiliated unions, including SITRATERCO, on themes including self-esteem, gender, occupational health, human rights of women, leadership, and globalization. Each workshop included about twenty-five to thirty people; about a third of the workshops were for women only.[13]

In her autobiography, Domitila Hernández, a member of the *Sindicato de Trabajadores de la Empresa Agrícola Santa Ines* (Union of Workers of the Santa Ines Agricultural Corporation; SITRAESISA), a union of Dole workers in the Aguán Valley, recalls her first skittish encounters with the SITRATERCO women: "Because I was a rank-and-file officer they sent me to a workshop in La Lima, but I blew off the trip and told them I wasn't feeling good. But that wasn't it; I was afraid. I thought that I was going to lose my job." Later she did attend a seminar on parliamentary procedures in San Pedro Sula. "That was where I got into my head how important it was to be a rank-and-file union leader. Now it would be hard to stop being one." Soon after that the SITRATERCO women themselves traveled to Domitila's town "to explain to us what a Women's Committee is and what it's for. Then we organized ourselves into the Executive Committee of the Women's Committee." SITRAESISA's women then elected officers and members of their Women's Committee and launched a successful struggle for its inclusion in their union's bylaws.[14]

By this point the SITRATERCO veterans had honed their skills at presenting workshops. Typically a workshop went for one or two whole days, on paid company time, which led to a certain holiday atmosphere. Each workshop began with speeches of welcome and exhortation, then a ritual of introduction in which one participant introduced another comrade or read a little card on which she or he had written her or his expectations for the meeting. The rest of the time alternated between formal presentations by the leaders and breakouts into small groups, in which three to five participants were assigned a topic to discuss or a task to perform. A representative from each group would then present its findings before the whole. It was all designed to promote rank-and-file women's experience in public speaking in a safe context, as the more experienced women modeled leadership, helped other women practice it, and integrated men, if present, into debates on women's issues.[15]

Interspersed with the formal elements were games, known as *dinámicos*, designed to get participants up on their feet, laughing, and enjoying themselves as a group. Usually these games had an instructional subtext. One classic *dinámico* is about the postman. Everyone sits in a circle, with one person standing up in the middle. The person standing announces, "The postman comes and brings letters for everyone with black shoes," to use one example, and everyone with black shoes has to get up and change chairs. But there's one chair lacking, so whoever doesn't switch fast enough is left in the middle to announce a new category. In the process everyone inevitably hoots with laughter as they scramble for seats. Leaders, when they are in the center, use the game to introduce issues relevant to the workshop theme. Iris Munguía tells of one time she announced: "The postman comes and brings letters for everyone who thinks they're beautiful," and she was the only one who stood up—underscoring her subject of women and self-esteem. (This game also produces an entire genre of off-color humor. Zoila Lagos, while in the center, once giggled, "I'm not going to say what I was thinking..." and later revealed she had been tempted to announce, "The postman comes and brings letters for everyone who had sex last night." Another leader actually proclaimed: "The postman brings letters for everyone who isn't wearing any underwear."[16])

ALL IN A DAY'S WORK

To get a better feel for these workshops we can step inside a one-day COSIBAH workshop on May 5, 2001, entitled "*Necesidades Prácticas y Estratégicas de las Mujeres, Division Sexual del Trabajo*" (Practical Necessities and Women's Strategies, The Sexual Division of Labor). It was a sweltering hot day, as usual, in the banana town of Sabá in the Aguán Valley. SITRATERCO's Gloria García and Mirian Reyes, plus Zoila Lagos, a COSIBAH staffer, had arrived the night before after a five-hour trip from the Sula Valley. By 8:30 a.m. the thirty women participants, all over twenty-five, had also made it to the meeting hall in the back of Sabá's *Museo de Bellas Artes* (Museum of Fine Arts). Despite its impressive-sounding name, the hall was a simple structure without even a chalkboard to write on, and the women lined up eagerly on its old wooden benches with the paint wearing off. They, too, had traveled a long way to get here, by bus and the unions' pickup trucks from plantations all over the north coast.[17]

Domitila Hernández—by this point secretary of women for the local host union, SITRAESISA—opened the workshop by greeting the visitors, followed by Alirio Antonio Garay, SITRAESISA's president. Each participant then introduced herself and said where she'd come from; after each one, the rest of the participants applauded and welcomed her. "The workshop was tense at the beginning," Zoila commented in her minutes; "but as time passed the women relaxed and started sharing their stories and finally they realized that when women start talking about our own issues the time always flies."[18]

Mirian Reyes, secretary of organization for SITRATERCO at the time, started off the main body of the workshop with a *dinámico* involving girl dolls: each woman drew a picture of a doll, described its attributes, and the others had to guess who the drawing depicted. Mirian then identified patterns in the participants' descriptions of women. In Zoila's words:

> The conclusion drawn through this exercise was that the partici-
> pants realized that women, since we're so busy attending to the
> needs of others, almost never pay attention to our own needs;
> we don't think of ourselves, we don't pay attention to ourselves,
> we deny ourselves the right to exist for ourselves alone. The situ-
> ation is even worse when we try to bring up our own issues.[19]

After that the women numbered off into three groups charged with identifying the "resources and benefits" available in their communities, their households, and their unions. Together they came up with lists of concrete resources and designated whether men, women, or both controlled each one. Their unions, they noted, had chalkboards, e-mail, and radio programs, for example; their homes, televisions and couches; their communities, clinics, football fields, kindergartens. Women only had access to a few of these. Soon a discussion broke out of men's resistance to women's empowerment. "The men are always saying women are incompetent." "Bosses or husbands refuse permission to go to the workshops." "Her husband doesn't want her to open up her mind."[20]

Next it was time for a break; union helpers arrived with boxes of soda pop bottles and paper plates with little cakes on them. When everyone was together again, Gloria and Mirian had the women number off into four new groups to analyze the situation of women union officers, "bearing in mind the factors that influence banana production in the country and indicating which are practical and which are strategic necessities for women leaders." The groups reported back with a list of growing pressures from their packinghouse jobs: "Our salaries aren't adjusted." "They demand more production." "Women get sick more often." "There's age discrimination against women." They developed a list of concrete goals and solutions as well: "Conquer the fear of confronting the bosses." "Raise self-esteem." "More participation by women in the executive committees and in important union decisions—and make sure those decisions benefit women." "Demand that our union contracts contain clauses that directly benefit women."[21]

Zoila then gave a talk about the big political-economic picture affecting banana production. She traced changes in access to the European market and explained how the banana transnationals were jockeying for position, resulting in massive layoffs and increasing instability in the labor market. Then she pulled back to talk more broadly about how the politics of neoliberalism were making Third World countries poorer every day—with devastating effects on women, in particular, ranging from the growth of the informal economy to increasing illiteracy and domestic violence. Meanwhile, she noted, structural adjustment programs mandated fewer and fewer State services. Focusing in on Honduras, she outlined a range of specific legal rights guaranteed to women and children. She asked the participants to write down "benefits and limits" available to women under the Honduran Labor Code and other legislation. The women responded by observing how legally-mandated vacations gave women the chance to rest, for example, but didn't pay for the time off. The law against domestic violence gave women the opportunity to denounce abusers, but not all women knew about it.[22]

Now it was lunchtime and they all relaxed with a plateful of the classic food of Honduran banana workers: chicken, rice, beans, salad, and fried plantains; they washed it down with locally produced watermelon, pineapple, and melon juice. By this point it was maybe 105 degrees in the hall. But the women were also well aware that they were having a rare day off from working in the packing-houses—and that the companies were paying for their time.[23]

After lunch, moving closer and closer in on concrete measures, Mirian had them return to their original lists from the morning, of resources available in their unions, communities, and homes, and asked them to brainstorm on how to take advantage of them.[24]

Then the workshop took up a new theme, the sexual division of labor in the home. Mirian asked each woman to write down all the tasks she performed in her household from when she got out of bed to when she went to sleep and the amount of time she spent on each. She then facilitated a general discussion on the long hours of housework. Afterward, she stressed:

> Consciousness raising should begin in our homes; we shouldn't just praise our male companions for their triumphs. We women are more responsible, even though we're taking on a double or triple role. It doesn't bother our male comrades or husbands when we work and contribute our wages to household needs.... Men shouldn't be so bothered by our participation in organizations. What we can do is influence them to accompany us in our activities.

Mirian underscored the importance of validating domestic labor and of gradually incorporating the rest of the members of the family in housework.[25]

By this point the day was getting long, but after another snack the women enthusiastically kept right on into the early evening. In one last exercise Mirian returned, again, to their first group exercise. She gave each participant six colored note cards and a felt pen and had them write down again who had access to each of the community, union, and household resources they had named previously. Compiling their lists together, the women then constructed a list of "practical necessities" and "strategic necessities" in each sphere, including "valuing housework" and "equitable participation of women" in important household decisions. The women concluded that in their unions they should "take part in decisions and add clauses and demands that benefit women. And by helping women grow, strengthen our organizations." All this, they said, would require that women educate themselves and "gain their own autonomy."

The workshop ended with another of the games that had been interspersed throughout the day, getting all the women up on their feet and laughing. Then they all dispersed for the long, hot, bumpy trip home.[26]

In their evaluations at its conclusion, the participants described the workshop's impact eloquently:

In these seminars you open your eyes and learn a lot.

I learned that we women can use politics in any space we find ourselves in.

I learned that the work that's done in the home has a lot of value, and we have to begin to appreciate it, starting with ourselves.

We have to demand that they send us to workshops like this one, because when you're here, you wake up.

My husband was wrong. They didn't brainwash me in this workshop like he said they would. I learned to value my work.

I'm committed to reproducing what I learned here.

What I learned in this workshop was to share with other women comrades and that I am exploiting my body to demand so much work from it, without rest.

They made us think about how important we women are, in our homes, union, community, and work.[27]

All that in just one day.

A NEW UNDERSTANDING OF GENDER AND WOMANHOOD

Hurricane Mitch initially knocked COSIBAH, like everything else, off its feet. For a long time the federation's energy went entirely into disaster relief, as did SITRATERCO's, then to supporting the unions in their post-Mitch battles with Chiquita and Dole. Eighty percent of women affiliated with COSIBAH were initially unemployed. Six hundred—around a fifth—had not regained their jobs as of 2000, and most of those never got their jobs back. The devastation of women's activism in SITRATERCO after the hurricane, moreover, was replicated in the other unions. "In each union, there were five or six women who pushed; afterward often only one," recalls Iris.[28]

But COSIBAH and its institutional support for women's work survived undiminished. After Mitch the federation's projects, in fact, expanded. During the first three years after Mitch alone (1999–2001) COSIBAH sponsored forty-two different conferences and workshops. Twelve of them were all-women, with titles including:

Emotional Recuperation and Self-Esteem

Sex, Gender, and Strategic Planning

Duties and Rights

Administration and Basic Accounting

The Global March of Woman

Sex-Gender and Domestic Violence

Sexual Division of Labor, Practical and Strategic Necessities[29]

The core of the enterprise remained the same: transforming women from timid, passive, and isolated individuals to self-confident, informed activists. COSIBAH's manual for workshops on self-esteem offers a glimpse into that process. It starts with a "magic dozen of self-esteem" on the first page, including "Be able to accept our strengths and weaknesses," "Know that everyone has something that makes us feel proud," "Accept that everyone is someone important," "Liberate ourselves from guilt," "Act according to what we want, feel, and think without worrying about other people's approval," and "Above all, find the courage to *love ourselves* as the unique beings we are" [emphasis in original].[30]

After defining self-esteem as "the appreciation and consideration that people have of themselves," the booklet runs through a whole series of questions—which the facilitator presumably presents to the participants:

Why is self-esteem important?

What is self-esteem for?

How is self-esteem formed, and how does it matter in our lives?

How can we boost self-esteem?[31]

The answers, in turn, echo many of the themes laid out in the "magic dozen." They begin by asserting that society and culture condition women not to value themselves or their work. The COSIBAH manual distinguishes itself from more individualistic arguments for women's liberation, however, by moving quickly to validate connections between individual women and their social and cultural contexts. Self-esteem is important, it declares, so that "we can know that we're valuable and that others are, too." Every human being carries inside her or him "three worlds":

MY THREE WORLDS

1. ME: The world inside each person.

2. ME and mine: the world of relationships between myself and the people closest to me.

3. ME, MINE, AND THE WORLD that surrounds us and the social context that I and the other people inhabit.[32]

From there the manual moves to link individual self-esteem seamlessly to a greater knowledge of, and most importantly, transformation of the world around them. Through self-esteem "we gain more knowledge about things that we didn't know about before, for example health, work, education, and rights, among others." Women can boost self-esteem "by searching for better ways of thinking and acting as people with rights and abilities" and "promoting situations and spaces that allow for the development of the humanity that we carry inside us." The authors include a testimonial from a woman that sums up perfectly the connection between self-respect and social change:

> Before I didn't feel so important.... Before I didn't have the courage to start up a conversation with other people; I thought they'd reject me. Now I relate to everyone in my town—with the mayor, with the judge, with the people that work in the registration office, with the salespeople, well, with everybody and even with others that aren't from here.[33]

The manual also includes a section entitled *"Apuntes Sobre Identidad Femenina"* (A Few Points on Female Identity), written by Marcela Lagarde and provided by the *Centro de Derechos de Mujeres* (Center for Women's Rights) in San Pedro Sula. "Our identity is constructed through a socio-cultural historical process," the section explains, "and it assigns each person an identity, that is, they tell us what gender we belong to, what class, what nationality, what age, and much more." For each one of these, it continues, we're taught a determined conduct—such as "woman (gender)=weak."

> Patriarchal society considers a woman to be a product of nature (ignoring the socialization process). It considers women to be weak, fragile, stupid, incapable, mothers, sacrificing wives, because of our vagina, ovaries, breasts, hormones. It says "if we're born that way," that's how we act. We're reduced to our instincts; for example, maternal instincts—but they never talk about paternal instincts. Or they say menstruation makes us act crazy.[34]

Rather than feel vulnerable and weak, Lagarde insists, women should claim "independence, a thirst for knowledge and life." The manual concludes by exhorting that women should "change ourselves into mothers, but of ourselves."[35]

As well as disseminating this kind of powerful critique of traditional gender roles, by 2003 Iris and other COSIBAH staffers were also training emerging women leaders in the federation's seven affiliated unions to lead workshops they themselves had previously attended—replicating SITRATERCO's earlier model of snowballing empowerment. In August of that year, they ran a "Second Workshop on the Continuing Process of Team-Formation." Asked to form themselves into two groups and choose names, the participants came up with "The Invincibles" and "Women Educators of the Future." The Invincibles were assigned the theme of sex and gender, and the Women Educators of the Future, self-esteem. Each group then spent two days designing, presenting, and then getting feedback on a workshop. When it was over, each participant took home with her not only the manual on self-esteem described above but also a handout on how to integrate a gender focus into unions, tips on communication and popular education techniques, song lyrics to "*Hermano Dame Tu Mano*," "*Venceremos*," "*Si se Calla el Cantor*," and "*Gracias a la Vida*," and her own healthy dose of self-confidence as a woman ready to return to her own union and run workshops herself.[36]

If powerful all-female workshops like this one were designed to bring about a transformation of rank-and-file women banana workers in particular, the majority of COSIBAH's workshops were mixed gender, such as one entitled "The Labor Movement: Its Advances, Difficulties, and Perspectives From the Point of View of Women." Many of these mixed-gender workshops did not address gender directly but integrated women into mainstream educational training of rank-and-file union members on themes such as parliamentary procedures, literacy, or media work.[37]

Through all this COSIBAH has replicated SITRATERCO's model of women's self-transformation, supporting a new generation of women leaders in the other seven unions. The results have not been as spectacular as in SITRATERCO—in 2003, only two women served as secretary of women, and none in other upper-level offices—but all the unions have Women's Committees and women now hold office at the plantation level for the first time. It's a slow process of education, leadership development, and changing union men all over again, this time throughout Honduras.[38]

REACHING OUT, DRAWING IN

As the list of participants in the 1996 First National Conference of
Banana Women suggests, COSIBAH has also proven to be a bridge
to local women's organizations outside the banana sector. Zoila Lagos, who works with Iris Munguía on the COSIBAH staff supporting women's projects, embodies these links and the widening circle
of banana women's activism—which, as we will see, soon expanded
far beyond Honduras. Zoila was born in 1952 in San Pedro Sula, to
a very poor family. She grew up listening to *Radio Rebelde* from Cuba
and says it was the music she loved so much that first made her a radi-
cal. She had her first child at thirteen, got married "to the first idiot
I met," and had two more children in her teens and early twenties.
Eventually she left the abusive relationship, went back to school, and
worked for fourteen years as a nurse for the national social security
health system. She emerged as a leader in the health care workers'
union in the 80s, while also getting deeply involved in Left politics,
to the point where she had to flee in exile to Mexico City in 1988.[39]

When she returned in 1991, Zoila started getting interested
in women's issues for the first time—at the same moment the
SITRATERCO women were running their first Sunday-afternoon
workshops. That year she attended the first national feminist conference of women in Honduras, on issues of sex and gender, and
formed a women's group in her neighborhood addressing issues of
domestic violence. Through this work Zoila was invited to attend a
training on domestic violence at the *Centro de Derechos de Mujeres*
in Tegucigalpa, and eventually went to work at the organization's
branch in San Pedro Sula. Much like the banana women, she committed herself to developing as an educator and started leading
workshops all over the area, including, by 1995, working first with
SITRATERCO's women and then with COSIBAH's. When, in
the aftermath of Mitch, the Tegucigalpa women's center lost much
of its funding, changed priorities, and laid Zoila off, Iris gradually
hired her for more work at COSIBAH. By 2001, Zoila was working full-time with Iris.[40]

Zoila brings many virtues to COSIBAH: not only a joyful per-
sonality and a painstaking dedication, but a breadth of vision from
her Left background that widens the women's political understand-

ing. Her skills at facilitating and training are highly developed, she's widely read, and she voraciously hunts down materials from all over the world to use in COSIBAH women's work. Perhaps most important, her long experience in the Honduran women's movement helps the banana workers imagine their own goals in wider terms.[41]

Since 1999, Iris Munguía, Zoila Lagos, and COSIBAH have expanded the federation's women's work into a new range of projects. In part, they're reaching out to women beyond the banana sector; in part, they're thinking even more deeply about how to address the challenges facing banana women, such as the lack of employment opportunities after they leave the packinghouses. In 2003, as part of a larger grant, COSIBAH obtained $2,000 from a German nonprofit to set up sewing classes to train women to make custom clothes. First they bought sewing machines and hired a teacher; then, every Sunday for three months, ten women between the ages of twenty-eight and forty, mostly single, from plantations all over the region, met in SITRATERCO's cinder-block labor school building, upstairs from COSIBAH, in La Lima. As always, it was difficult for the women students to squeeze out the time, especially given their irregular work hours in the packinghouses. One Sunday only four could make it because the day before, the *corte* (cut) on one plantation had stretched from 7 a.m. until 8 p.m. Using other grants, COSIBAH has also sponsored classes on making candies and baked goods.[42]

At the same time COSIBAH is increasingly involved outside the banana sector. In 2003, Iris and Zoila joined Norma Rodríguez, a longtime campesina activist, and her partner, Fidel Reyes, to help set up a women's pig-farming cooperative near Omoa, on the coast near the Guatemala border. They are helping twelve poor women learn to run their own collective "microenterprise" as a model for women's independent economic activity.[43]

GENDER MEANS MEN TOO

To fully capture women's work in COSIBAH in the early 2000s, though, we have to bring the men into the story, because individual men's support for, and engagement in, women's projects is also key to its success. Take Nelson Nuñez, the organizer who handed out that gender pamphlet to the maquiladora workers, for example. Nelson, born in 1965, grew up on a banana plantation and learned to fight for his rights from a militant union father and a Leftist school teacher who taught him never to forget where he came from. When he was nineteen he started working at Finca Guaruma II, near La Lima. Very quickly he rose within the union ranks to secretary general of his plantation committee. In 1989 he got a three-year grant to learn union education techniques. When he returned to the plantation even more deeply committed and militant, he was fired, beaten up by company agents, and jailed. Only after a big battle was he eventually reinstated in his job. In 1997 he started working as an educator and later organizer at COSIBAH.[44]

Nelson is a fun character, whose sense of humor and flirtatiousness mask a militant dedication to organizing. He represents a newer generation of banana union men, who came up through the ranks after women were in the leadership and who see women's empowerment as part of the normal work of trade unions. Liz O'Connor, who worked for the AFL-CIO in Honduras when Nelson was first hired as an organizer, remembers her work with him on a project organizing women and new workers (an example of the new, post–Cold War solidarity work of the AFL-CIO): "It was very pragmatic. It wasn't 'we're going to target women, because they're extra oppressed,' but 'we want to win.' If you're going to win, you can't ignore thirty percent of the workforce."[45] Yet, of course, earlier generations of union men had. Nelson serves as an important figure supporting women's trade union activism and, just as an important, helps legitimate the women's analysis of gender politics within that project.[46]

The success of Oneyda Galindo testifies to Nelson's labors and the hard work of all the COSIBAH staffers. Oneyda, a single mother of five kids in her early forties, spent fifteen years working on a nonunion Chiquita-owned packing plant outside El Progreso. In 2000 and 2001, she emerged as the natural leader of a union drive on her plantation. Meanwhile she attended COSIBAH workshops on leadership development and on domestic violence. In October 2001 Oneyda and her coworkers formed a new union, now known as SITRASURCO (*Sindicato de Trabajadores de la Agropecuaria Surco*; Union of Workers of the SURCO Agroindustrial Company). In February 2004, after months of complicated negotiations and legal maneuvering, she signed the union's first contract with Chiquita. She is now the union's president, and the first woman president of a banana union in Latin American history. "I'm not shy," she explained, when asked what it was that made her so special.[47]

José María Martínez, known as "Chema," is another example. Chema, in his late forties, spent twenty-two years working on Finca Cobb, eleven years working on union radio programs, and now serves as director of communications for COSIBAH as well as public relations director for SITRATERCO. Chema, too, is tremendously hardworking and, like much of the staff, loves to send around joke e-mail cards to his coworkers and friends during his lunch break. Chema helps run four banana union–sponsored radio programs, which broadcast from all over the north of Honduras and to which he buzzes around on a COSIBAH–owned motorcycle. *Sindicalista del Aire* (Trade Unionist of the Air) plays Mondays through Saturdays from 7:15 to 8:00 p.m. out of El Progreso, *Reportero Popular* (People's Reporter) three days a week in the Aguán Valley, and *Reportero Sindical* (Union Reporter) Mondays through Fridays in the Olanchito Valley. He also runs a program for newly organized sugar cane workers. Mixed-gender teams of "people's reporters" manage the shows nightly.

The programs are enormously popular: *Sindicalista del Aire* alone reaches three thousand listeners every night—in part because the program lists times at which workers need to show up at each *finca* the next morning, but also because the shows are extremely participatory. Not only do both women and men train to manage these shows and produce reports, but hundreds call in to the live shows to send birthday greetings, alert fellow-workers to contract violations by a given manager, or protest about a comrade who was fired unjustly before his or her probation period was over. Family members in the United States even call in with live messages.[48]

Through these radio programs Chema, like Nelson, brings women's issues into the unions' mainstream, further legitimating them in the process. He regularly announces women's activities in

the unions, brings Iris and other women onto the shows, and dis-
cusses women's concerns, while drawing women producers and reporters into radio work. Chema further legitimates women's work
in *Nueva Visión Sindical*, COSIBAH's official full-color newsletter,
which comes out about twice a year. The April 2002 issue, for
example, included an article on labor unions and globalization,
the column *"Nuestra Gente"* (Our People) featuring a profile of
a rank-and-file man, reports on three affiliated unions, a spread
on the 1954 general strike, *"Conquistas de la Mujer Hondureña"*
(Conquests of the Honduran Woman), an article on a pioneer
woman in the 1954 general strike, a report on the visit of Danish
trade unionists, a two-page spread called *"¿Qué Es Eso de Género?"*
(What's That About Gender?), and portraits of two martyrs from
Honduran labor history.[49] Chema also works tirelessly on behalf
of women's specific projects in COSIBAH. In August 2003, for
example, he could be found cutting out pink construction paper
in the shape of a women's symbol for a big poster for an upcom-
ing regional women's conference—completely unfazed, as if this is
what all good union men do.[50]

The women's final important male ally is German Zepeda,
president of COSIBAH. As one of the most powerful figures in
the Honduran, indeed Latin American, banana labor movement,
and a rock-solid supporter of women's work, he is crucial to the
women's success. German Zepeda's father was a railroad brakeman
for Chiquita; German himself worked as a welder in a banana pu-
ree plant. While working full-time he hammered out two years
of college and first emerged as a trade union leader in the sugar
cane processing sector. After becoming a SITRATERCO member in 1989, he rose quickly to its executive committee and, in
1994, spearheaded the founding of COSIBAH and became its
president.[51]

German is the big strategic thinker behind COSIBAH. Like
Iris, he's a smart listener—you can almost see the little wheels going
around in his head behind his eyes. He's also a master at grasping
the big political-economic picture in the global banana industry.
Most important for our analysis here, men and women in the banana labor movement respect him immensely, and he is completely
supportive of women's work at every turn. Like other key male

supporters, German became active in SITRATERCO well after women had already established the secretary of women and the *Comité Femenino,* well after it became accepted that women would be leaders, and he carries that culture into COSIBAH's leadership. Moreover, German also sees the big picture of how embattled the unions are in their relationship with the transnationals and, crucially, understands that women's work makes all the banana unions stronger in that relationship.[52]

CONCLUSION

Posters, pamphlets, pig farms, radio programs, and new union contracts, not to mention the first woman president of a banana union—COSIBAH in the post-Mitch years has produced a quiet flurry of women's empowerment and creativity—the payoff for the long, hard labors in SITRATERCO. Male allies have helped bring women's work to the very center of union work. Yet COSIBAH also allows for autonomous projects where women do not have to answer to potentially hostile union officers from their individual unions. At the same time, this higher level of *women's* work—casting a broader geographical net and drawing in a broader set of allies—depends on a higher level of *union* solidarity. In the banana unions of Honduras, in other words, women's power is part and parcel of union power.

The surprise, perhaps, is that this extraordinary movement emerged in such a seemingly unlikely place. After all, it was Nicaragua, El Salvador, and Guatemala where the great insurgencies of the 1970s and 80s emerged. The reasons are complex. During the 1960s and 70s the Honduran labor movement, along with Costa Rica's, was the strongest in Central America, with the banana unions at its forefront. Honduras didn't, though, produce a rebellion like those in its sister countries during the 1970s and 80s—in part because more advanced agrarian reform absorbed resistance, in part because its unions were seriously compromised in these years by AFL-CIO domination. Equally important, when the insurgencies of the other three countries broke out, the US swiftly moved in to occupy Honduras for use as a military base for the Contra War, spending millions training Honduran troops and developing infrastructure, such as Palmerola Air Base near the Nicaraguan border. (The country even became known as "the U.S.S. Honduras.") Left activities that did emerge in Honduras were summarily repressed.[53]

Ironically, in contrast to workers' organizations in the other Central American countries, including Costa Rica, devastated by the wars and counterinsurgency programs, the Honduran labor movement emerged from the end of these conflicts in the early 1990s largely intact. During the 1990s SITRATERCO and the other Honduran banana unions nonetheless struggled to survive plantation closures, new production systems, and other machinations of the banana corporations—not to mention Hurricane Mitch. But they survived the political storm of the 1980s in far better shape than their sister unions. In the same years, union women in Honduras were able to learn from, be inspired by, and link up with women's struggles in Nicaragua and El Salvador that were far more developed than those in the relatively quiescent Honduras. The two key elements of COSISBAH and SITRATERCO's women's projects—strong unions and strong women—can thus be understood only in a long-term perspective involving all of Central America, as well as its would-be master to the north.

Chema Martínez and Belkis Castro, COSIBAH staff, La Lima, Cortés, Honduras, August 2003

Participants in COLSIBA conference, Puerto Cortés, Honduras, September 2004; Digna Figueroa (SITRAPROADASA, Honduras), Nineth Méndez (ASEPROLA, Costa Rica), Adela Torres, (SITRAINAGRO, Colombia), Carla Quinto (SITRAINAGRO, Colombia), Reina Sabina Orellana (SITRAESISA, Honduras); seated in front: Berta Gómez (FETRABACH, Nicaragua) (left to right).

CHAPTER FOUR

Latin America
The Big Challenge

In early September 2004, thirty-one women banana workers from across Central America along with various allies gathered in a pleasant beachfront hotel in Puerto Cortés, Honduras, for a women's conference of the *Coordinadora Latinoamericana de Sindicatos Bananeros* (Coalition of Latin American Banana Unions; COLSIBA). Two came from Colombia, four from Nicaragua, one from Ecuador, three from Guatemala, two from Panamá, one from Costa Rica, and seventeen locally from Honduras. For the next four days they met in the hotel's big, wide conference room. This time they had air-conditioning (although it tended to blast cold air across half the seats). During the first day the women, who'd all brought copies of their unions' contracts with them, broke into groups to compare clauses in their contracts regarding women's particular concerns like maternity leave and equal pay. They identified clauses already in place in some of the contracts, then strategized about which they wanted standardized across their seven countries and three transnational employers.

Over the course of the next few days, the women heard a presentation from Nineth Méndez, a consultant from Costa Rica, on flexible labor systems; another on the Central American Free Trade Agreement (CAFTA) from Edgar Lara, a professor from El Salvador (who traveled roundtrip from San Salvador by bus just to give a three-hour talk); and got to go on a tour of the port itself, the largest in Central America. No banana ships were loading that morning, but the women got to see a warehouse of cardboard boxes just arrived from China, minerals being loading off to Europe, and a gargantuan container ship carrying maquiladora products bound for Houston. At night they strolled up and down the only slightly garbage-littered beach, went out dancing a few blocks down the road, or lolled about in their rooms watching TV. The second night Chema Martínez from COSIBAH commandeered the phone in the hotel's tiny office and hooked it up to a live broadcast from *Radio Progreso*. The women from each of the visiting countries took turns speaking about the current situation of the banana unions and women's projects in their respective countries.[1]

After the four-day conference was over, while we were both waiting around the COSIBAH office for our rides home, I asked Telma Gómez, a young rank-and-file activist in SITRASURCO, the new Honduran Chiquita union, what her favorite part of the conference had been. Without a second's hesitation, she shot back: "The presentation on the free trade agreement. Now I really have it down."[2]

Telma Gómez's preference for political economy over partying, along with the Puerto Cortés conference itself—taking place in a logistical hub of the global economy, with women present from seven countries, addressing a sophisticated mix of themes blending gender equity, global labor systems, and union power—exemplify the full, transnational scale of Latin American banana women's activism by 2004. Now our story, like Telma's understanding of global trade politics, crosses the Honduran border and moves onto an even broader stage, both geographically and strategically, and the full breadth of the banana women's achievements becomes clear—along with the sobering realities they still face.

Starting in the late 1990s women banana workers' activism has expanded throughout Central America and into Colombia and Ecuador through another new body, COLSIBA. Just as COSIBAH unleashed women's work in Honduras, COLSIBA has created new opportunities for connections between women banana workers throughout Latin America. By the turn of the millennium COLSIBA women had used that institutional opening to construct a new, powerful transnational identity as *mujeres bananeras en lucha*—banana women in struggle—and to project women's empowerment within the unions onto a much larger sphere.

The challenges facing women's work in COLSIBA, however, have been much greater than in COSIBAH, the stakes far higher, as the by-now experienced and self-confident women of Honduras and the northern countries encounter unions with little precedent for women's equality or even participation. The women's situation, though—and along with it COLSIBA's—is changing fast.

COLSIBA is itself an unprecedented achievement, the product of new global strategic thinking on the part of trade unions. German Zepeda recalls, "Logically, there was a big problem with the banana labor movement in Latin America. We'd never met. Even at the level of individual countries, we had so many unions and didn't even know each other."[3] In May 1993, leaders from banana unions in Honduras, Guatemala, Nicaragua, Panamá, and Colombia first met informally with Costa Rican banana unionists in San José, Costa Rica to strategize support for its embattled banana unions. Out of that meeting emerged COLSIBA (Ecuador joined in 2000). In all of Latin America, COLSIBA is the only organization that joins unions in the same sector across national lines in an autonomous regional coalition. COLSIBA delegates, usually one or two top leaders from each country, meet several times a year, rotating the location, to share knowledge of corporate practices, the global banana industry, and all-important trade policies in Europe; and, most important, to strategize joint responses and campaigns. When crises emerge in a given country—a strike, for example, or the Del Monte kidnappings in Guatemala—COLSIBA leaders are quick to travel to the region, launch international press campaigns, and link up with allies. COLSIBA has been especially important in supporting union organizing campaigns in Ecuador.[4]

One of COLSIBA's great achievements has been the 2001 agreement with Chiquita, brokered through the International Union of Food Workers, in which the corporation pledges to respect worker rights. The agreement not only institutionalizes COLSIBA as the body representing banana workers throughout a broad swath of Latin America, but it provides a vital, if ambiguous, tool for protecting and advancing the banana unions. Since 90 percent of unionized banana workers in Latin America work for

Chiquita, the agreement can be invoked if the corporation engages in anti-union behavior at unionized plantations—thus helping stabilize COLSIBA affiliates' always precarious existence. It also protects workers' basic right to organize new unions at plantations owned by or subcontracting from Chiquita.[5] Chiquita's willingness to countenance organizing contrasts sharply with the other big banana corporations' active hostility.

The unions affiliated with COLSIBA diverge dramatically in their relative power, political stances, and the position of women within them. It's hard to grasp them all at once, but we can at least sketch out the big picture, all the more complex because, with the exception of Honduras, the most powerful unions aren't necessarily the most advanced on women's issues.

At one end of the spectrum lies Honduras, with its 10,000 union members and advanced gender politics.[6] Its closest approximation, in terms of women's empowerment, is Nicaragua. Two union federations—the *Federación de Sindicatos Bananeros de Chinandega* (Federation of Chinandega Banana Unions; FETRABACH), and the *Asociación de Trabjadores del Campo–Trabajadores Bananeros de Nicaragua* (Association of Farm Workers–Banana Workers of Nicaragua; ATC)—together represented a total of 5,000 banana workers in Nicaragua in 2003.[7] As in Honduras, many women banana workers in Nicaragua have a highly developed consciousness on women's issues. Distinct activities for women are understood to be part of the movement; both federations have secretaries of women and their executive committees are evenly split between men and women. Yet some of the most entrenched, unbending banana union men in all of Latin America still hold power in Nicaragua. Even more important to understanding the situation in Nicaragua, the working conditions for men and women alike on the unionized plantations—all independent producers that sell to Chiquita—are atrocious and pay close to starvation wages.[8]

Near the Atlantic Coast in Morales, Guatemala, the *Sindicato de Trabajadores Bananeros de Izabal* (Union of Izabal Banana Workers; SITRABI), represented 2,833 Del Monte workers in 2004.[9] With one very powerful exception, Selfa Sandoval, women are absent from its leadership, but Selfa and her allies regularly offer women's programs. The *Unión Sindical de Trabajadores Guatemaltecos* (Labor Union of Guatemalan Workers; UNSITRAGUA), affiliated with former guerrillas, represents another 3,200 banana workers at Chiquita as well as some at Dole.[10] While individual women can be strong presences within it, UNSITRAGUA participates in COLSIBA only sporadically.[11]

In terms of women's presence in banana unions' leadership, it's all downhill from there. In Costa Rica, secretaries of women and women's workshops are an established presence, but women participate only marginally at other levels of leadership. Its once-enormous banana unions, 18,000 strong in 1980, were destroyed by *Solidarismo* in the late 1980s and today only have contracts covering about 2,000 workers.[12] In Panamá, by contrast, unions at Chiquita remained powerful until quite recently, when the corporation sold off its holdings in the Puerto Armuelles region, in part to avoid union obligations. The remaining 3,600 unionized workers enjoy excellent contracts, but women's presence within their unions has historically been meek. When COLSIBA first met in Panamá in 1996, one Honduran woman participant was horrified to see that the women present "only cooked the food." Since then, secretaries of women have been established in some unions, opening space for women's activities on a small scale.[13]

Colombia and Ecuador, finally, represent the furthest extremes of banana unionization. Colombia has the largest number of banana union members of all, with 17,500 workers in the *Sindicato Nacional de Trabajadores de la Industria Agropecuaria* (National Union of Agroindustrial Workers; SITRAINAGRO) in 2004. They enjoy excellent contracts with independent producers and at former Chiquita-owned plantations recently sold off to BANACOL, a large national producer. The Colombian unions have survived, even grown, despite hideous repression. Since 1991 two thousand trade unionists have been assassinated in Colombia, including many members of SITRAINAGRO; of the twenty men who founded the union in 1978, only five are still alive. The union's current leaders only survive because of twenty-four-hour armed protection and an ambiguous truce with the paramilitaries.

Within this context of repression, women's presence inside SITRAINAGRO is marginal. Colombian women have had to struggle to be hired in the packinghouses in the first place. Less acculturated to boldly take risks in the face of repression, and more likely to be the sole supporters of their children when menfolk have been assassinated, women have not been active in the union's leadership, with only a few exceptions. In 2003, Adela Torres, serving as secretary of women as well as secretary of organization for her region, was SITRAINAGRO's only woman among the sixty-five union officers. Women's projects and workshops are an accepted practice among the rank and file, however.[14]

Ecuador, lastly, is a nonunion nightmare. None of its approximately 250,000 banana workers are protected by a contract, and those who try to unionize are fired, threatened at gunpoint, blacklisted, or all three. The *Federación Nacional de Campesinos e Indígenas Libres de Ecuador* (National Federation of Farmers and Free Indigenous Peoples of Ecuador; FENACLE), which represents agricultural workers in Ecuador, has been trying very hard to organize banana workers and gain even a single contract in the banana sector. A wide range of international allies have come to its aid; but the situation remains bleak. Within FENACLE itself, women are not particularly empowered. A series of women have worked for FENACLE on organizing projects, but the union's leadership remains all-male.[15]

Overall, despite the fact that they constitute one-quarter to one-third of banana workers and union members in all these countries, women have been shut out of most union power and governance, their issues rarely raised before 1995. That year, when the unions were surveyed, and still in 2004, women in most countries served only as secretary of women, if there was one. Today in Guatemala, Colombia, Nicaragua, and Honduras they do hold other positions, but only in Honduras and Nicaragua does more than one woman serve among the dozen or so officers at the top. The challenge facing COLSIBA's women and their allies is stark—and in every country, the unions themselves at risk.

A WEB OF WOMEN

But that's only the bad news, and by no means the whole story. COLSIBA has not only strengthened all its affiliated unions tremendously, but made possible significant changes in their gender politics and provided the platform for sophisticated women's projects beyond even the achievements of the Hondurans.

When COLSIBA was first formed in 1993, all the leaders present were men. In contrast to COSIBAH, founded in Honduras a year later, COLSIBA's initial bylaws contained no mention of women's work. Two years later, when the federation held its Third Regional Conference in San Pedro Sula, Honduras, women were present for the first time: Mathilde Aguilar Quiroz, at that point representing Costa Rica; Doris García and Lillian Sandoval from Nicaragua; and Iris Munguía from Honduras. Together, they worked out thirteen "Resolutions on the Theme of Women," which they presented to the conference. Four resolutions targeted employers and their governments, demanding strategies to address discrimination against women on the plantations, including lower salaries, limited access to housing and employment, long hours, and the firing of pregnant women. The rest of the resolutions spoke to their union comrades. They asked for the creation of secretaries of women; they wanted education and training programs for women unionists; they asked the unions to support regional interchanges between them. They politely suggested that all union publications deal with "women's issues." Most broadly, daring to state their fullest vision, they asked their comrades to:

> Stimulate debate (in congresses, assemblies, educational programs, meetings, etc.) in our organizations regarding discrimination against women, so that we can advance a better understanding of the problem and move toward a culture of respect and equality between men and women.[16]

Concretely, the women presented a proposal creating a secretary of women for COLSIBA. With two powerful men—German Zepeda, president of COSIBAH, and Gilberth Bermúdez, president of the Costa Rican banana union federation—supporting it openly, the proposal passed without a ripple. Iris Munguía was named the new secretary of women and formally installed in the position in Puerto Barrios, Guatemala, in 1996.[17]

COLSIBA's door was now open for women's work, but what lay beyond was seriously daunting. "I was really afraid to accept the position," Iris recalls. "It was hard to talk to the men at the

Latin American level."[18] Just as they had in COSIBAH, women within COLSIBA started out with a self-study, gathering brief reports from each country on the status of women banana workers, their labors, their priorities for activism, and their position in the unions.[19] Just as they had in Honduras, they next organized a conference—but in this case, just for the women, in Chinandega, Nicaragua, in November 1995, under the theme "*Ámbito de los Derechos de Mujeres Bananeras*" (The Climate for Banana Women's Rights). With the same mixture of proud celebration of accomplishments and sober tackling of realities that would characterize all their work, the delegates used the conference both to honor gains already achieved in each country and to focus in on a set of key priorities to pursue, mostly within their specific national contexts.[20]

That Chinandega conference launched, in turn, a series of more or less annual conferences of union banana women in Latin America. The conferences rotate, as do COLSIBA meetings, among the affiliated countries, but are autonomously controlled by the women, who choose the themes, location, and format of each meeting. These conferences in many ways form the core of COLSIBA women's work, and their evolution over the years reflects the growing knowledge, self-confidence, and breadth of the banana women's transnational project. In the early years COLSIBA women's conferences concentrated on challenges the women faced in their packinghouse work and on demands for inclusion in their unions, as had the women's first 1995 resolutions. Between 1997 and 1999 their conferences added a focus on occupational health, through a project funded by the Danish labor movement. Then, in 2000 and 2001, the banana women turned to two special projects: an extensive self-study of women banana workers and collecting their own life stories.[21]

By 2002, COLSIBA women began to move outward to the international context of the banana women's situation, using their conferences to educate themselves about globalization while always keeping the connection to gender issues, their own lives, and their unions. In every case COLSIBA women, like COSIBAH's, continued to integrate women's specific concerns with broader union struggles. They headlined their poster for a 2002 conference on the Free Trade Area of the Americas (FTAA) and Plan Puebla-Panamá (PPP), a giant US-sponsored infrastructure project extending from southern Mexico to Panamá, "*No Mas Control ni Apropiación de Nuestra Región*" (No More Control or Appropriation of Our Region)," linking women's demands for control over their own bodies with demands for regional economic sovereignty.[22] Their August 2003 conference, "*Jornada Sobre Estrategias y Técnicas de Contratación Colectiva*" (Workshop on Strategies and Techniques for Collective Bargaining), similarly moved seamlessly from discussions of how to negotiate with the corporations during collective bargaining over a contract, to how to negotiate with one's male partner over permission to leave the house, to how to negotiate women's equality within the unions.[23]

By the 2004 COLSIBA women's conference in Puerto Cortés, Honduras, they were able to integrate with ease seemingly disparate presentations on CAFTA and flexible labor systems with a gender-based discussion of how to standardize clauses regarding women's concerns across the whole region. The women of COLSIBA were able to cast a broad political net while solidifying their specific demands as women banana workers and unionists. In only nine years, in other words, through their work with COLSIBA, the banana women had moved from cautiously looking at their own daily lives to understanding the broadest of global political-economic processes, without ever losing sight of the challenges at home and in their unions.

The growing intellectual and political breadth of COLSIBA women was clear during their 2002 "*VII Encuentro Latinoamericano de Mujeres Bananeras Frente a las Estrategias de Apertura Comercial: ALCA, TLC's y el Plan Puebla Panamá*" (Seventh Latin American Conference of Banana Women Taking on Trade Liberalization: the FTAA, Free Trade Agreements, and the Plan Puebla-Panamá). Held in San Pedro Sula, Honduras, from August 29 to 31, the conference brought together two women from Colombia, seven from Nicaragua, four from Guatemala, one each from Costa Rica and Panamá, and thirteen from Honduras. Chema Martínez, from COSIBAH, served as master of ceremonies; allies present included Juan Funez, secretary-general of the *Federación Independiente de Trabajadores de Honduras* (Independent Federation of Honduran

Workers; FITH); Rolando Mateo, an educator working with the
FITH; representatives from support groups for maquiladora workers; and a representative from the Honduran sugar, honey, and
allied workers' union.

The topic of trade agreements was, no question, a daunting,
technical one for everyone involved. Minutes from the workshop
show that María Eugenia Ochoa, the facilitator, began with a
brainstorming session to get everyone's starting point out in the
open, asking the participants, "What do we already know about
the theme? What do we want to know?" Soon she moved into
a more lecture-style presentation on the content of the different
trade agreements and the broader politics of trade. Then the participants broke into groups by country to discuss and answer a
series of questions on topics such as health, housing, education,
employment opportunities, labor rights, popular culture, the
environment, sports and recreation, and access to technology.[24]
The exercise shows the banana women moving not only toward
an understanding of complex trade politics, but effective collective action—while at the same time envisioning a different society.
On the question of housing, for example, when the women put
together all their responses they concluded:

> What do we have now? High cost of living that makes it inac-
> cessible. Salaries are very low. There isn't housing with dignity.
> Housing is borrowed or rented.

> What do we want and need? That the government has plans for
> public housing. Just salaries to buy housing. That the govern-
> ment builds houses and sells them at low cost.

> What does the Plan Puebla-Panamá propose? Privatization of
> services.

> What position do the women workers take? That funds exist for
> public housing. Women's unity to demand rights to housing.
> That the PPP considers housing projects.[25]

By the conference's end, the participants had developed a series
of *pronunciamientos* (pronouncements) on behalf of women banana
workers, about the damaging effects of structural adjustment programs, free trade agreements, and the PPP's model for development.

They proposed instead, "Social and economic policies that guarantee a dignified life for the people of Latin America, especially women, who have felt the greatest impact of neoliberal policies at all levels," along with respect for ILO labor conventions—especially regarding the right to organize and bargain collectively—and an end to privatization of public services. They demanded that all decisions about trade, development, and international loans "be decided through a process that is participatory and transparent." Their declaration concluded: "We're not against regional integration; we're against its imposition. Another model for development is possible!!!"[26]

Beyond their political and intellectual content, the banana women's conferences also provide a much-needed space for women in the leadership of each country to meet regularly and support each other. Most of these women are extremely isolated. When they go home, they are under tremendous pressure to perform both as union leaders and as women's advocates—as well, usually, as heads of their households. At a conference, together for three or four days at a time, in the same meeting room and modest hotel, they get to gossip, bond, give advice, get advice, relax, and, in general, replenish their emotional and intellectual resources for another six or nine months of hard labor. The sheer joy of these conferences overflows: the women greet each other on arrival with the deepest of camaraderie; they sing, they tell jokes, they tease, they drink beer, they dance, they go swimming, they do a little shopping. And they strategize about how to take on the hard questions of empowering banana women and confronting their enormous problems.[27]

Selfa Sandoval, from SITRABI in Guatemala, is perhaps the most embattled and isolated of them all. Selfa is a laughing, energetic, tough cookie, who remains powerful in her union because she works hard and fellow rank-and-file members know it. She holds office both as secretary of women and secretary of organization, press, and propaganda on the executive committee for all of SITRABI. She also serves as grievance secretary of her subsection. Selfa is thus one of the three or four highest-ranking banana women in Latin America. But some of the men who lead her union are not happy about this at all. They're quick to try and thwart Selfa or to spread nasty gossip behind her back. Selfa flourishes, though, because of support she gets from women in the other countries. Only five hours from La Lima by bus, she's geographically the closest of the non-Hondurans to the women of SITRATERCO and COSIBAH. Like all the banana women leaders, she is still in a long-term process of self-transformation, aided by her COLSIBA networks. In the fall of 2003 Selfa ran for mayor of Los Amates, near Morales. Although she landed far back in the pack, she emerged from the experience even stronger and more confident of herself and of her constituents' faith in her.[28]

COLSIBA delivers for rank-and-file women as well. Iris Munguía, Gloria García, Zoila Lagos, and Domitila Hernández's trip to Morales, Guatemala, in 2002, in which experienced women leaders reached out to younger women across national borders to deliver an analysis of domestic violence, serves as a classic example. The day after the Morales workshop the four women gave the same workshop for twenty-four UNSITRAGUA members in Puerto Barrios, an hour east on the coast. For local participants the arrival of powerhouse women from Honduras or other countries is a big event. Not only do local leaders get support, but rank-and-file women interact with compelling role models who consciously groom the younger women for self-empowerment and leadership. ("Are you going to be the next secretary-general of your union?" a leader might suggest to a particularly attentive participant who she's noticed from a previous event.) Additionally, because the COLSIBA women's conferences rotate to each of the countries, local rank-and-file and lower-level leadership women get to participate, further reinforcing the chain of mentorship.[29]

Catalina Pérez Querra from Puerto Barrios, Guatemala, serves as a good example. She works on a Chiquita plantation near Puerto Barrios represented by UNSITRAGUA. Catalina is the only woman of the seven people on her local union's governing body. In 1994, when she first started working with the union, "it was really hard to…confront the *patrón*," she says. But over the next eight years, she was invited to COLSIBA workshops—one in Nicaragua, two in Honduras, another in Costa Rica. All that made it possible for her to hold her own in dealing both with union men and with management. "I feel happy because the *compañeras* have given me this space to be in the union." Like many of the banana workers in Guatemala, Catalina doesn't know how to read or write, but, she announces shyly but proudly, "Now that I'm in the union, I've learned a lot. I can write my own name."[30]

COLSIBA women's interconnections and travel, in turn, have supported women's work in banana unions at the national and local levels. While women's projects in the other countries are nowhere as developed as in Honduras, they are growing. In Guatemala, for example, SITRABI organized a 2003 workshop in celebration of International Women's Day and wrapped up a year-long sewing class completed by thirty-four women. On a more modest scale, Ligia Lamich Meléndez, secretary of women for a small union representing Chiquita workers in Puerto Viejo, Sarapaquí, Costa Rica, reported in July, 2004 that her union had offered classes for women in computers, labor rights, and sewing undergarments. The most ambitious project began in late 2004 in Colombia, in SITRAINAGRO, under the direction of the *Escuela Nacional Sindical* (National Labor School). Focusing on the theme of "*derechos laborales sexuales y reproductivos de las trabajadoras bananeras*" (the labor, sexual, and reproductive rights of women banana workers), the campaign included workshops in four rural municipalities in the Urabá region, regional-level seminars, a conference in Medellín, and a broad nationwide media campaign—involving radio, photography exhibits, jingles, and popular musical figures. As well as women banana workers' reproductive rights, the campaign defended Colombian women's basic right to even work in the packinghouses, at risk in that country.[31]

WRITING THEIR OWN STORY

In addition to this rich world of leadership development, networking, and support for national-level women's work, COLSIBA women, beginning in 2000, took on two larger projects that illustrate how quickly their abilities were expanding and how broad their strategic thinking had become. The first was an extensive regional self-study of women banana workers in all the countries affiliated with COLSIBA, completed in July 2001 as a 110-page report entitled *Diagnóstico Participativo con Enfoque de Género Sobre Condiciones Sociales, Económicas, Laborales y Organizativas de las Mujeres Trabajadoras Bananeras* (Participative Analysis with a Focus on Gender Regarding Social, Economic, Working, and Organizing Conditions for Women Banana Workers). Here, as with their initial, brief self-study, the COLSIBA women were replicating their approach in Honduras. But this time the task was much more complex, given the geographical span, enormous national differences, and participants' disparities in education.[32] The report was explicitly designed to further the interests of women banana workers within their unions. As one of their advisors put it in the report's introduction, "This type of action-investigation has a political goal at its base that will permit COLSIBA through its national coordination of women to propel and broaden its presence and organization at both the local and national levels."[33]

From the start, the banana women and their allies consciously designed their *Diagnóstico* to be as much about their process of conducting the study as about the final product. Women packinghouse workers from leadership to rank and file got to learn how to conduct a formal, social-scientific investigation, in the process developing new skills, raising their political consciousness, and increasing their intellectual self-confidence. Each of the COLSIBA affiliates put together an investigative team for their country: one or two women union leaders, two or more rank-and-file activists, and a university-trained facilitator. Together, each team conducted interviews with managers, union leaders, and government officials; researched available printed documents; and wrote a report on conditions in their country. At a March 2001 workshop in San Pedro Sula, Honduras, the participants compiled all the material from the different countries into a final overall report. All told, 175 people participated in the project, seven of them men.[34]

The minutes of the project's final workshop capture beautifully individual women's empowerment through the project. When asked on the evaluation form how she felt about the process, one woman replied, "At first I felt fears and doubts. Later optimism and a sense of teamwork." Another, evidently a facilitator as well as participant, responded: "I felt very satisfied at having pulled off the job and in coming to know that we women have a great capacity to achieve many things." Another, evidently also a facilitator, confessed: "At first I felt a little afraid. Later, as my women comrades were obtaining the information, we felt a great deal of satisfaction. I also felt enthusiastic and a little anxious about reaching the final stage." Summing up the experience, in response to the next question—"What did I learn? What did I teach?"—one participant wrote, "I learned about the methodological steps and structure of an analysis with a focus on gender.... I taught that the level of academic training doesn't matter when there's a desire and knowledge through experience and when there's the will to work as a team."[35]

The study itself first documents the number of women banana workers in each country and demographics such as age and marital status. It then turns to specific issues facing the women: hours of work, housing situations, options for other employment, transportation—all the issues examined earlier. In the report's conclusion, the women go out of their way to stress a broad definition of "women's work":

> All the people who participated accepted and developed the idea of analyzing women's housework from the perspective of WORK—and not a job—a perspective that presumes a more integral vision that includes both remunerated (productive) labor and nonremunerated (reproductive) labor.[36]

The report's second half takes up women's situation in their different unions, with country-by-country details. Overall, the *Diagnóstico*, produced by the union women themselves, is a pioneering study of women banana workers in Latin America.[37] In 2002, with funding from the Danish labor movement, COLSIBA women condensed the report into a forty-two-page pamphlet with illustrations, entitled *Mujeres Trabajadores Bananeras: Desafíos y Esperanzas* (Women Banana Workers: Challenges and Hopes), and the accompanying five-page *Agenda Regional de las Mujeres Bananeras* (Banana Women's Regional Agenda), and distributed both throughout COLSIBA's affiliates.[38]

The second project was a book of their own autobiographies entitled *Lo Que Hemos Vivido: Luchas de Mujeres Bananeras* (What We've Lived: Struggles of Banana Women), published in 2003.[39] The book emerged from a 2001 conference at which the women decided to write their own life stories.[40] They "knew that the

women weren't in the labor history of their countries' unions," Iris
Munguía recalls, and wanted to record their autobiographies to
make sure, especially given banana women's lack of literacy, that
their stories didn't disappear.[41] Then, working with ASEPROLA,
an academically-trained group of facilitators from Costa Rica,
COLSIBA women devised a set of life-history questions which individual women answered during workshops at the national level.
In the book's introduction, Iris stresses how therapeutic it was for
the women to write their stories down:

> Each one of us lived to be able to revive those memories and
> have the courage to open our old wounds, facing up to the
> ghost of a past asleep but not forgotten, and in the process of
> disentanglement and remembrance we were able to discover our
> sorrows and successes. Writing each paragraph was like return-
> ing to relive it, and each painful moment brought new tears,
> tears that were clean, healing, and needed.[42]

"OK, we've got all these stories," Iris remembers thinking; the
question was what to do with them. They decided to make a book.
The women got a grant from the Danish labor movement; $3,000
from Trócaire, an Irish Catholic charity; and ASEPROLA donated
technical support. Together with Ana Naranjo and Alvaro Rojas
from ASEPROLA, the banana women selected the stories of fourteen women from five countries, ranging from a desperately poor
migrant worker in Costa Rica with little access to unionization to
two of the most experienced SITRATERCO veterans.[43]

The editors very consciously constructed the book as a celebration of women banana unionists' collective history and memory.
It opens with an anonymous quote from a woman banana worker:
"The participation of women in the unions' many struggles has
been important, but we've disappeared from them, because we
haven't told our own history."[44] The book is dedicated to Emilia
Hernández, "la Rápida" (the Fast One), the heroine of the 1954
Honduran general strike whose picture hangs in the SITRATERCO
office today, "and, through her, to all the banana women." Emilia
had told her son, Manuel, after the strike, "I have done it for your
children and some day the workers are going to be thankful for it."
The dedication replies:

With this publication we want to answer affirmatively to Emilia. Yes, the workers of the banana plantations of all Latin America thank you for your sacrifice, and that of thousands of women that have struggled, day after day, for the most sacred rights of the men and women workers, for equality, dignity, and social justice.[45]

Together, the COLSIBA women's book and their self-study illustrate quite how much the banana women have developed since 1985 and the first stirrings of women's activism in SITRATERCO. Through COLSIBA, women banana unionists have constructed a powerful collective identity that crosses lines of plantation, union, nation, and education. It's constructed not only through the cross-national travel the women enjoy, the workshops, and in the historical memory captured in their autobiographies, but also through little things like posters from their annual conferences, or the zippered coin purses, tote bags, and key chains they carry home with them, like the coffee mug commemorating Mother's Day, May 2003, with a message Zoila and Iris wrote up:

Tú eres alguien Especial,

Tú eres una gran Mujer

Porque tienes la valentia de aceptarte y quererte como eres.

(You are someone Special

You are a great Woman

Because you have the courage to accept yourself and like yourself the way you are).[46]

POWER AT THE BIG TABLE

If the women's independent activism is thriving within COLSIBA, its upper reaches, however, still remain predominantly male, and the challenges facing women banana union leaders formidable. Picture, for example, the afternoon of November 15, 2003, in Chinandega, Nicaragua. Iris Munguía, Gloria García, and Domitila Hernández have just attended a mixed-gender workshop on domestic violence with rank-and-file members of FETRABACH, at the local Sandinista-affiliated women's center. During the lunch break, their Nicaraguan hostesses announce "a little surprise." A seven-piece band pops up, and a young girl dressed in long white ruffled skirts with red and black trim performs three folk dances. Four hostesses, now bedecked with tissue-paper crowns and their own brightly colored long skirts, perform the ceremonial dance of the Festival of San Roque, which, they explain, traditionally honors the festival's organizers. During the dance, the four Nicaraguans drag the three Honduran women (plus a visiting North American) to the group's center, top them with the crowns, present them with gifts wrapped in shiny green cellophane paper, and twirl them about. Eventually, all the participants join in for three rounds of dancing. For everyone present, it's a moment of great joy and celebration. Afterward the three Honduran "queens," still in their crowns, sing and laugh in their pickup truck across town to a COLSIBA meeting.

There the whole tone changes: it's dark and serious in the room, the power politics are palpable, and for the rest of the afternoon, Iris sits at one end of the table alone with the top male leaders, arms crossed on her chest, unsmiling, calculating the exact moment she might play her cards. The rest of the women cluster at the other end of the table, largely out of the conversational loop. Needless to say, the crowns stay in the truck outside. The contrast between the women's playful, bright, independent camaraderie and the challenge of entering COLSIBA's upper reaches could not have been starker.[47]

To most COLSIBA meetings, each country sends two delegates, and, with the exception of Honduras and sometimes Guatemala, they have usually been men, chosen by national-level male leaders who themselves attend. Its coordinator and sub-coordinator have always been men. One woman's presence at the top is constitutionally guaranteed, however, by the official inclusion of the secretary of women in its three-member executive committee, along with the two top officers.[48]

Some men from the banana unions outside Honduras remain extremely resistant or even overtly hostile to the women's thrust for equality. In 2002, one female national-level leader from outside Honduras confided, "The men are still afraid of women's leadership. We've learned a lot and we've advanced. The men don't want to give up the power."[49] In Panamá, the situation was so bad in the mid 90s that the position of secretary of women was actually held by a man, who refused to meet with representatives from the union's Women's Committee.[50]

But most men in the banana unions' leadership are not hostile. More common is a vague, passive acceptance; or a certain indifference, potential antagonism or resistance held in check by supportive men and the growing legitimacy of women's presence. Then there's a third group, which the women refer to as *aliados* (allies): male unionists who can be counted on for support at key moments. The Honduran men top the list, but the other unions are crisscrossed with men, at many different levels of leadership, who will come through for the women. "Don Arnulfo" is one. At the 2003 Chinandega, Nicaragua, workshop at which the dance took place, I was encouraged, or more accurately instructed, to take photographs throughout the meeting.* Initially I focused on the women leaders and on rank-and-file participants, male and female. "Take a picture of Don Arnulfo, take a picture of Don Arnulfo," Berta Gómez, secretary of women for FETRABACH, kept insisting. I wanted to ignore her; I hadn't, I thought, come to focus on the one male leader present. But obediently I snapped a close-up of the shy, warm, modest-looking Don Arnulfo—who, it turned out, was the only man among seven leaders elected to the local union's new executive committee. He was a classic *aliado*, and Berta was teaching me to appreciate him.[51]

Overall, women are steadily gaining within COLSIBA. While Iris felt it was once difficult for her to talk with men at the Latin

---

* Throughout this project I was very conscious of the politics of being a North American white woman taking pictures of Latin Americans. But the politics of photography turned out differently than I had anticipated; once again, the banana women weren't passive victims at all. They brought their own cameras, too, and repeatedly asked me to take their pictures with mine, sometimes competing with each other to be in the photographs. On three occasions I was specifically instructed to send copies of the pictures I'd just taken. Twice I was told I should get a digital camera so I could send the pictures by computer; on several other occasions, it was suggested I develop the pictures locally so they could see them. And all along they were taking photographs of me, too.

American level, "now it's easy," she affirms. "Now, I have *lots* of credibility with the women *and* with the men. I can feel that support when we have a meeting with men; I can feel that the men are waiting to hear what Iris is going to say."[52] Early documents produced by women in COLSIBA have a tone of careful deference. Their 1995 *Acuerdos de la III Conferencia Latinoamericana de Sindicatos Bananeros* (Agreements of the Third Conference of Latin American Banana Unions), for example, included phrases like "to encourage with all due respect" or "to respectfully urge" before calling for such measures as mechanisms that facilitate the greater participation of women or the establishment of secretaries of women in their statutes.[53] By the early 2000s that tone was gone, in a slow but startling process of deep cultural change. "We women are in the process right now of learning how to go about changing our cultures," reflects Iris. "For hundreds of years, our culture has always told us that unions are for men only, in a culture in which all the organizations are made up of men."[54]

Union democracy is a key variable in women's advancement. It's not just by chance that women are most empowered in the banana unions of Honduras, which have a deep level of union democracy. In SITRATERCO, for example, women can participate actively and with considerable power in plantation-level committees, regular union assemblies, and as elected officers at three different levels, as well as on the Women's Committee. Perhaps most important, all offices have four-year term limits, which produces an ongoing turnover in the leadership—regularly opening up space for both women's demands and for their individual and collective entry into power, while giving all members a stake in widespread union education. In many of the other countries, by contrast, the unions have no term limits, and in some cases elections can be few or far between. Even in those unions with a great degree of internal democracy on paper, actual practices can still keep women out. "In our organization the structure doesn't allow women the vote in general assemblies," observed Selfa Sandoval of SITRABI in 2004. "They do have a voice but not the vote, and that's where the problem comes in; women haven't occupied a full-time office on the executive committee, because the majority of the officers are men." Recently, though, after the formation of *cuadros* (teams) of women within SITRABI with the help of ASEPROLA, COLSIBA, and other allies, the situation has changed dramatically. "Before we only had three women in leadership positions, but using this new approach we've been able to get fifteen women into the union leadership," Sandoval points out.[55]

Strategically, women banana unionists in each individual country are using COLSIBA, the international body, to leverage power for women in the unions of their home countries. COLSIBA, along with the powerful example of Honduras, legitimates the presence of women in the different national unions and guarantees them a certain presence at the top when they're at COLSIBA meetings, even if they lack similar power at home. This plays out especially clearly in the politics of who gets to go to meetings. By tradition, each national-level federation sends one or two delegates, depending on funds and availability, and each picks its own delegation. COLSIBA has an unwritten policy, frequently invoked, of not interfering in an affiliate's internal domestic affairs. Usually this has meant that women don't get sent as delegates and the COLSIBA leadership can't officially object.

At a COLSIBA meeting in San José, Costa Rica, in January 2004, though, the women were strong enough to introduce a new rule that each country send one woman and one man—successfully evading the "don't interfere" tradition by merely establishing gender policy.[56]

Who gets to attend COLSIBA meetings, in turn, sets up powerful information politics. If only men, plus one or two women, have access to international meetings, they retain a monopoly on vital knowledge not only about what happened in the meeting, but of the larger picture of corporate strategy, markets, trade regimes, and the international labor movement. Continuity matters, too. When a woman is present at just one meeting but doesn't have any background, the experience can be intimidating or disheartening. Iris observes:

> When they're discussing hard problems, even more when they're discussing questions that maybe we women don't understand very well—for example, when the banana market is discussed, or free trade agreements, or tariffs, that automatically are pretty difficult—sometimes the women come up short in terms of information. If we don't have the information to talk on a given theme at a meeting, we aren't going to speak up.[57]

These information politics can be quite intense. In one instance, a top male leader from the country hosting a COLSIBA meeting didn't even tell local women leaders, including the secretary of women of his union, about the meeting until the day before.[58] At a broad level, if women are not at COLSIBA meetings, they lose the ability to participate in future decisions and think strategically in a well-informed manner. Conversely, if they have been able to attend a COLSIBA meeting in another country, they return home as carriers of vital knowledge and are in turn further empowered as leaders at home.[59]

The women have effectively addressed these information politics, though, by establishing their own parallel channels of knowledge. Through conferences, travel to women's workshops, friendships, and information-gathering projects they have created an alternative sphere that complements and in part compensates for their exclusion from full equality within COLSIBA. For example, a woman might not have been present at a COLSIBA meeting that discussed European trade regimes, but she might have attended the women's own three-day workshop on globalization.

Last, and not by any means least, COLSIBA women have gained access to their own independent money.[60] COLSIBA regularly receives outside funding specifically earmarked for women's projects. Money sent for Latin American–level women's projects—such as the *Diagnóstico*, the collection of autobiographies, or regional conferences—flows directly from funders to Iris Munguía, giving the women full autonomy to develop their own priorities, politics, and projects at the regional level. Other funds have been earmarked for women's work in specific countries. These funds have usually been channeled through the different national federations' male leaders. Unfortunately, on occasion some men have spent all or part of the money for other purposes—such as when SITRATERCO leaders kept the ILO funds—rather than pass them on to the secretary of women or Women's Committee. But the situation here, too, is advancing. In August 2003, for the very first time, Iris Munguía was able to distribute grant funds directly to the women representatives of each of the different countries. It was a symbolic and powerful moment, if quotidian in its appearance. During the last day of the COLSIBA women's conference on negotiation in El Progreso,

Honduras, Iris quietly handed a woman from each federation an envelope with $1,500 in cash. When each woman returned home, the money was hers to control—with, of course, accountability to both local women and Iris.[61]

The politics of information, money, and gender converge especially powerfully around issues of technology and equipment—to which women banana unionists haven't had equal access, or often any access at all. Even in Honduras, activists reported during their 2001 self-study, at the level of the individual unions affiliated with COSIBAH, women "do not have any access to, and even less use of…telephones, fax machines, computers, desks, records," or even chairs, not to mention all-important cars. "This limitation is also associated with a lack of technical training on the part of the same leaders. They need to learn to drive cars, use office equipment, and work on computers." Just to complete the self-study, the women reported, they had to rent computers because they couldn't get access to those of their own unions. At region-wide COLSIBA women's conferences in the mid 2000s, the leaders present repeatedly reported that they hadn't been able to communicate with Iris Munguía or with each other because men colleagues denied access to basic equipment. Again, though, they're addressing the problem: In September 2004, Iris delivered to the secretaries of women from each of the affiliated countries the money to buy their *own* computers and pay for fifteen women to take a week-long computer class.[62]

By late 2004 COLSIBA's top women were, in several individual cases, starting to move beyond their male comrades in knowledge, leadership ability, and drive. Their tight support networks and alternative information channels are paying off. In their skills, self-confidence, broad vision, and growing knowledge of global economic affairs they are now the match of many male leaders in their unions and federations. Just as important, they often have a level of militance and energy that can surpass that of their male peers. These women see the big picture; they know the corporations are swooping down to pick their unions off, one by one; they know that their unions have to organize the unorganized, adapt new tactics, and tightly coordinate their strategies transnationally—or die. As individual women are ready to take the reins at the very top of their organizations, the looming challenge is whether male banana union leaders can accept—and even celebrate—women presidents and secretary-generals above them.

CONCLUSION

All in all, COLSIBA is an enormous achievement, both in its very existence and in its extraordinary and rapidly evolving gender politics. The enterprise, spanning seven countries, holds together across sprawling geographical distance, bridging spectacular organizational diversity, national cultures, and, not to be underestimated, widely divergent ideological tendencies and educational levels. Within the federation, women bring sharp strategic thinking as they struggle to establish a place, literally, at the table of international union solidarity, and to make women's concerns integral to the definition of union work at the international level—while at the same time protecting and nurturing each other for year-round work at home.

Just as women and their male allies used SITRATERCO in the late 1990s to level upward women's place in the banana unions in Honduras, so, in turn, has Honduras been the linchpin of the transformation in the 2000s of both COLSIBA and the national and union-level bodies of banana workers throughout Latin America. As the Puerto Cortés conference exemplifies, by 2004 the banana women's scope had expanded not just to embrace women banana workers across unprecedented geographical distance, but, through their autobiographies, self-study, and educational initiatives, to take on the largest of global economic processes and women's place in transforming them. That's why Telma Gómez could be so enthusiastic about understanding the Central American Free Trade Agreement—and about successfully combating it, too.

Clockwise from top left: Ligia Lamich, (SITRAGAH, Costa
Rica), Selfa Sandoval (SITRABI, Guatemala), Berta Gómez
(FETRABACH, Nicaragua), Luisa Paz Jiménez (ASEPROLA,
Costa Rica).

Toño, Jessica, Iris, and Ivan Munguía, La Lima, Cortés, Honduras,
November 2002 (left to right).

CHAPTER FIVE

The War at Home

For all their impressive activism, self-development, and expanding horizons, women banana unionists aren't superwomen. They come home at the end of the day, exhausted or exhilarated, to their own private lives, where there are dishes to be washed, children to raise, and, sometimes, partners to relax or argue with; and where the politics of gender among banana workers are played out on a more intimate stage. To more fully grasp their challenges as well as their joys, we can look at the personal side a bit more—at the women's relationships, family politics, and personal dynamics with the men with whom they are enmeshed.

At the core of the entire challenge facing women banana workers is the large Latin American cultural concept known as machismo. In its broadest meaning, machismo encompasses an entire package of patriarchy, sexism, and male self-importance that pervades Latin American society and culture. Machismo is institutionalized in the family and runs through male self-identity in public as well as private roles. Many Latin American men pride themselves on being "macho" and celebrate its combination of domination over women, sexual prowess, and strutting arrogance. As a 2001 report from banana women in Panamá put it, "Machismo and our cultures tell us that a women has to be obedient, submissive, and put up with whatever her husband or partner hands her, for better or worse."[1] Women banana workers, in their projects, are taking on this enormous cultural tradition at every turn. "*El no es machista*" (He's not a male chauvinist) is one of the highest compliments they can pay to a particular man. More often, they speak of gradations. As one longtime banana activist contrasted Honduran banana union men with those from other countries, "Here they're *machistas*, but there they're *supermachistas*."[2]

At a practical, personal level, one of the immediate forms male domination takes is that husbands and male partners believe that their womenfolk must ask permission to attend a meeting or even to leave the house. Nicaraguan banana women reported in the COLSIBA 2001 *Diagnóstico*, for example, that a key barrier to women's participation was "spouses' mistrust of their women; they don't allow them to participate."[3] Honduran women reported similarly, "Jealous husbands don't let them participate."[4] At their 2003 conference on negotiation and collective bargaining, women leaders spent more than two hours sharing tips on how to get out of the house when their men didn't want to grant them permission to leave (suggestions included just not asking for it and bargaining away something else).

The concept of machismo also justifies patriarchal divisions of labor in the family that, in turn, limit women's ability to be active union members. Male partners' resistance to providing child care, in particular, severely limits women's participation. On one occasion I was chatting with a male union activist—not a banana worker himself—at a banana union function. Just making conversation, I asked how many children he had. "Three," he replied. "Who are they with now?" I asked. "Their grandmother." "Do you help watch them?" "No." "Do you cook?" "No." "Do you wash dishes?" "No." "Why not?" I finally asked. "Porque soy *machista!*" he burst out proudly, his chest puffed out. (I put on my best charming smile and replied, "In the United States, we think men who cook and clean and wash dishes and take care of children are really sexy.")

Because male partners are so often resistant to women's independence and activism, it's not surprising that the vast majority of women banana union activists are single—although in almost every case they have children. "Those that participate are principally single women or a few women that are brave fighters," reported the Guatemalans in the *Diagnóstico.*[5] Oneyda Galindo from Honduras, the first woman banana union president, comments, "It's easier being single. I don't have to ask permission." In some cases, a separation from a partner has liberated a woman to choose union activity.[6] 'Antonia,' from SITRATERCO in Honduras, writes in her autobiography: "When I separated from my partner I got braver because I'm a unionized woman. Three months after I was separated from my partner, I started to take part in seminars and workshops in my organization [and] in COSIBAH." She concluded: "If I had been with my partner, I would never have done it."[7] In other cases the man is long gone—off to another relationship, another city, or another country. In still other instances, activists have had to deal with open hostility to their level of union activity. "Your husband tells you that if you keep it up, we're better off separating," reported one woman at the 2001 COSIBAH workshop in the Aguán Valley.[8] Iris Munguía's husband and the father of her three children once gave her an ultimatum: either give up union activism, or he would leave. She continued her activities; four years later he left for other reasons.[9]

A significant portion of women leaders, though, remain in marriage or what they call *uniones libres* (free unions, or common-law marriages). Most of these relationships remain largely rocky. Santos Licona, a leader in the new Chiquita union in Honduras of which Oneyda Galindo is president, says she has to ask her husband's permission to attend meetings, "and he always gets mad." He was injured in an accident and now only works intermittently as a vendor. She retorts, "I'm the one who's working, I'm the one whose lungs hurt, and I have the right to defend us. And he can't mess with my business on that front."[10] A few women privately described a variety of long-term relationships that allow for a degree of independence—because the man spends his evenings out of the house drinking, because they have a mutual arrangement to ignore each other but stay together, or because both lie to each other.

In the rarest of rare cases a woman leader enjoys a relationship with a male comrade who fully endorses her union activities and shares in housework. Asked if her husband supported her work, Berta Gómez, one of the top leaders in Nicaragua, replied enthusiastically, "Yes! He's an officer, too. He washes dishes, irons, and watches the kids."[11] The first time I met him, in August 2004, he was in the FETRABACH union office contentedly sewing a skirt for his daughter on one of the union's sewing machines.[12] Perhaps not coincidentally, all three of the highest-level banana women leaders in Nicaragua reported male partners that cooked, cleaned, and shared child care, a legacy, we can surmise, of feminist activism in the aftermath of the Nicaraguan Revolution.

The women's difficult choices produce an enormous amount of personal anguish. 'Luisa,' one of the SITRATERCO pioneers, writes that during the glory years of women's struggles in that union, "Through all this, the work in the union and on the Women's Committee that took up my time, I lost control of my children." Always in a hurry, working at both the packing plant and the union, teaching workshops on Sundays, "I never had the time to dedicate myself to them and enjoy a day with my children in the house, or go out for a walk. I regret not having given them all the affection that they needed in those years." But she concludes: "I believe that it was worth the trouble to be able to do what I wanted, without a husband to hold me back, to be able to struggle fearlessly. I was free from any pressures."[13]

The male peers of these leaders, also in their thirties, forties, and fifties, haven't had to choose between union activism and their families. With very few exceptions, they are married with children; their wives are not involved in union or political work of any sort; when they come home, dinner is on the table.[14] "I think that sometimes there's greater opposition to women's participation on the part of the same male union leaders," reported one Honduran woman in a 2001 workshop. "Just to give one example, I invited a woman comrade to a workshop…and her partner, who was also a leader, said to me, 'What did you invite her for?' Who was going to cook his food?"[15]

Given the available male partners—whether in the unions or outside them—and their attendant gender-role expectations, those women union veterans who are single generally aren't looking to marry or join households with a man. They say they are interested in men as romantic partners, and often have them, but consistently say marrying isn't worth the trouble, that is, all the domestic labor and subservience involved. If their choice to be single leaves them exhausted as "superwomen," balancing union work, wage work, and domestic responsibilities, the trade-off is freedom and the deep rewards of parenting and union struggle.[16]

The real long-term action in changing men is with their sons. The banana women are busily raising nonsexist sons. As Zoila Lagos reports from the 2001 Aguán Valley workshop, the women participants wanted "their sons and daughters to understand the importance and value of [housework], as part of a strategy to educate boys and girls to be less sexist and more sensitive to women's issues."[17] 'Emilia' recounts in her autobiography:

> Now that most of the family has grown up, the domestic labor is shared. While some iron their clothes and others make their beds, others sweep up. There's no difference between men and women because I had already received workshops on gender from the Women's Committee before I first had children, and that has helped me enormously, especially because now the men don't see the difference between washing a dish, hitting a ball, and studying.[18]

'Carmen,' a SITRATERCO veteran, similarly writes: "The housework tasks are shared by my children, nieces and nephews, and my mother. In my house there are only two women, my mother and me, with seven men. Everyone can cook, wash clothes, clean the house."[19] Not coincidentally, Berta Gómez of Nicaragua, when asked why her husband was so receptive to sharing housework and child care, answered, "Because his mother raised him that way."[20]

At the rank-and-file level, though, some women are resistant to disrupting gender expectations by raising men to take on "women's roles." In a deeply homophobic culture, many mothers are afraid of being accused of raising homosexual sons. Mirian Reyes recalls that at one of her very first SITRATERCO workshops on gender, one woman, the mother of sons only, walked out, announcing that she wasn't going to make them into "*maricones*," a derogatory term for homosexual men. (She came back, though, after she saw how much the other women were learning, and completed the workshop with great enthusiasm.)[21] The COLSIBA *Diagnóstico* speaks to this challenge: "We suggest that male children be involved more in domestic tasks, making them conscious that performing these activities doesn't make them lose their masculinity."[22]

Perhaps surprisingly, though, the women banana activists are not afraid of being called lesbians themselves. "The women don't mind if they call the women lesbians. But they *really* hate it if the men say their *son* is gay," Zoila Lagos observes. Most lesbians in the Latin American banana world remain deeply closeted, however, perhaps so invisible as to not be identifiable for either acceptance or attack.[23]

The story of one activist, though, reveals perhaps surprising acceptance and flexibility regarding gender roles in the banana unions. 'Marta Rodríguez,' thirty-six in 2003, works on a unionized banana plantation in Honduras, where she is one of fifty-four women among 280 men. 'Marta' identifies as a woman, dresses like a man, carries herself with a traditionally masculine swagger, and lives in her own house. For four years she lived with a woman partner who chose a traditional female appearance. During the late 1990s 'Marta' was twice elected president of her plantation's Women's Committee and in 2002 elected secretary-general of her entire plantation. Before her, women had only served as recording secretary. Management had one by one bought those women off, which made the union's men especially suspicious of female leadership. But 'Marta' reports that they are very supportive of her. They invite her to dinner at their houses, she says. "The men respect me. They don't think I'm a weak woman they have to take care of." In many ways 'Marta' has taken on the role of a male union leader, and been accepted in a way traditionally female activists aren't. Yet everyone knows she's a woman; and she participates actively in union, COSIBAH, and COLSIBA women's activities. She's certainly free to join in as she chooses. "In the union, I can do whatever I want without asking permission of anyone."[24]

Other women in the Honduran banana unions are aware of her sexual preference, and she's not the only rank-and-file woman experimenting with gender roles and relationships with women. Among activists 'Marta' is accepted as "one of the girls," even as she flirts openly with her female peers. At the formal level of women's activities in the unions, however, female homosexuality is evidently never discussed.

Among banana union activists, the rock-solid edifice of Latin American gender roles might not be falling down, but it has its fissures, and they are widening all the time. Raw patriarchal family expectations, machismo, and the institutionalized sexual division of labor keep thousands of women from participating fully in the banana labor movement of Latin America and cause enormous pain for those who do involve themselves. But activist women keep at it precisely because they *are* changing gender roles successfully, both in the formal worlds of COSIBAH and COLSIBA, as we have seen, and in their own private lives. They also know that their own sons will grow up to make some future comrades very happy.

Teacher and students at COSIBAH sewing class, La Lima, Cortés, Honduras, August 2003.

CHAPTER SIX

Global Allies

Throughout this story, outsiders—Germans, Danes, Costa Ricans, Americans—have appeared, providing money to the banana women, popping up to explain the Central American Free Trade Agreement, or helping analyze the complex intersection of class and gender in Latin America. Who exactly are all these allies? And where does the money come from?

Beyond the powerful networks established among banana workers themselves lies a dense thicket of outside allies ranging from middle-class Central American Leftists to the Danish labor movement to the Irish Catholic Church. Tracing the banana women's allies reveals the far-flung networks of global solidarity on which the banana unions draw, and of which most outsiders are unaware. It also helps unravel the complex interrelationships between union activism, international solidarity, and working-class women's empowerment in Latin America.

In Honduras, to begin, the banana women's most important allies have been women's groups within the national labor federations, within other social movements, or on the Left, such as the *Coordinadora Centroamericana de Trabajadores* (Coalition of Central American Workers; COCENTRA), a network of Central American labor unions founded in 1988, which has provided crucial support through its *Comité Femenino*. COSIBAH women also work closely with the *Centro de Derechos de Mujeres* (Center for Women's Rights; CDM) in San Pedro Sula, founded in 1992. The center initially focused on combating domestic violence in the mid 90s, and then in 1998 shifted to supporting maquiladora workers. Support and influence from other social movements and unions has flowed as much through individual activists as through formal organizational ties. Norma Rodríguez, for example, who has coordinated women's projects since the 1980s in the *Unión de Trabajadores del Campo*, a Honduran campesino organization, has met regularly with the Honduran banana women over the years. The same generation as the SITRATERCO pioneer women, Norma has imparted an experienced analysis of gender dynamics while also, like Zoila Lagos, serving as a bridge to a more explicit Left analysis of banana women's situation. Especially during the 1980s, a few individual women banana workers also developed leadership skills through contact with political organizations such as the *Movimiento de Mujeres Visitación Padilla*, a women's group that organized against US military bases in Honduras during the Contra War and provided support to trade union women.[1]

Middle-class and college-educated allies throughout Central America have also provided essential technical and analytical skills to the banana women. The men and women in Costa Rica who work with ASEPROLA (*Asociación Servicios de Promoción Laboral*), founded in 1985, travel regularly throughout Central and South America to assist COLSIBA and COSIBAH. Ana Victoria Naranjo Porras, for example, provided technical support for the COLSIBA women's self-study and edited their autobiographies; Ariane Grau and Alvaro Rojas also helped on the book; Luisa Paz Jiménez facilitated the women's 2003 workshop on negotiation and collective bargaining. Other middle-class allies volunteer as individuals with technical topics and facilitation, such as Ajax and Alex Irías in Honduras. In some cases these allies have specifically aided women's projects only; but just as often they enthusiastically serve the women as part of a broader commitment to supporting the banana unions in general.[2]

Perhaps surprisingly, in contrast to this wealth of contacts with local middle-class allies committed to labor solidarity, the banana women do not have a history of direct contact with the middle-class women's movement in Latin America. They did not, for example, participate in any of the groundbreaking feminist *encuentros* that began in Bogotá, Colombia, in 1981 and expanded through subsequent conferences in Peru, Mexico, Argentina, the

Dominican Republic, and elsewhere in Latin America during the 1980s, 1990s, and 2000s, uniting and inspiring women's organizations, grassroots activists, and feminist academics throughout Latin America. Asked whether she had had any relationship with the *encuentros*, Iris Munguía replied that she knew about them through e-mails and the Web, but that the banana women had never had any direct contact with them. Their organizational spheres apparently never overlapped.[3]

At the same time, though, there has clearly been a great deal of cross-fertilization between middle-class feminism and the banana women. Iris, Zoila, and other leaders voraciously borrow concepts, phrases, and technical approaches wherever they can find them, and their sources include a variety of materials and ideas produced by middle-class feminists. The poster for their 2002 "*VII Encuentro Latinoamericano De Mujeres Bananeras*" on the FTAA and PPP, for example, not only utilized the new term *encuentro* to describe a women's conference, but featured quotes from Alda Facio, a Costa Rican academic feminist, which Iris found on the Web: "*Las mujeres hemos sido globalizadas en la invisibilización, en la explotación, en el cuerpo, en la violencia, en el silencio, en la familia*" (We women have been globalized in being made invisible, in being exploited, in our bodies, in violence, in silence, and in the family) and "*Necesitamos más mujeres en el poder, pero también necesitamos que esas mujeres no sean cualquier mujer, sino personas dispuestas a luchar contra la globalización*" (We need more women in power, but we also need those women to be not just any women, but people committed to the fight against globalization).[4]

Indeed, the banana women have come so far, so fast in part because they haven't had to reinvent the wheel. They have been able to draw on flourishing women's activism and feminist consciousness in Latin America that was in place before they even started in 1985 and that has continued to develop apace since then. Take, for example, the pamphlet *Conozcamos de Género*, written by Zoila Lagos and Iris Munguía, that COSIBAH and COLSIBA have been distributing since 2003 throughout the banana unions—the one Nelson Nuñez handed out to the visiting maquiladora workers. The pamphlet includes concepts such as the distinction between sex (biologically constructed) and gender (socially constructed), expressed in phrases such as "We're born with our sex, but gender is learned," that were developed in academic contexts in the 1970s and 80s and have since flowed freely across national and class lines.[5]

Since the late 1990s the banana unions have also received enormous aid from allies in the United States and, especially, Europe. In Europe, a network of NGOs (nongovernmental organizations) known as Euroban has developed to explicitly support banana workers. Its affiliates include Germany's Banafair and Great Britain's Banana Link, which publishes the *Banana Trade News Bulletin*, a semiannual summary of labor and industry news. Euroban has been especially concerned with the situation of small producers within former European colonies and with promoting fair trade bananas; Banana Link, in particular, has proven a crucial bridge between Latin American banana unions and progressive Europeans and was the driving force behind a 1998 global conference on bananas.[6]

In the United States, the US Labor Education in the Americas Project (US/LEAP) has played a parallel role in publicizing the issues facing Latin American banana workers, but with a much more explicit focus on the banana labor movement. Along with European allies, it mobilized outrage over the 2002 attacks at Los Alamos in Ecuador and provided solidarity for the SITRABI Del Monte workers kidnapped in Guatemala in 2001, for example. US/LEAP is especially adept at pressuring the US government and US-based transnationals to guarantee labor rights for banana workers. It has also worked hard to try to stop the assassination of trade unionists in Colombia.[7]

Where is the AFL-CIO in all this? In 1997 President John Sweeney's administration finally kicked out the Cold Warriors lurking in its International Affairs Department, abandoned the AFL-CIO's anticommunist project in Latin America, abolished the American Institute for Free Labor Development (AIFLD),[*] and created an all-new body, the American Center for International Labor Solidarity, based in Washington, DC, that, for the most part, channels true solidarity to the labor movement in Latin America.[8] The AFL-CIO still has not publicly apologized for its decades of imperialist intervention in Latin American labor, and a debate currently rages regarding the federation's role in the 2002 attempted coup against Venezuelan president Hugo Chavez.[9] But in the past ten years it has consistently supported the banana unions of Latin America with solidarity and organizing support. When the Del Monte leaders fled Guatemala in 2001, for example, the AFL-CIO, in collaboration with the International Union of Food Workers (IUF), arranged short-term jobs for them as organizers with the Hotel Employees and Restaurant Employees Union (HERE) and other federation affiliates.[10]

The AFL-CIO, US/LEAP, European trade union allies, and COLSIBA all work closely, in turn, with the IUF, based in Switzerland with a Latin America office in Uruguay. The IUF, with COLSIBA, negotiated the all-important 2001 Chiquita Agreement.[11]

WHO PAYS THE BILLS?

All this aid falls under the category of solidarity. But Northern allies also directly fund the banana unions. The *Specialarbejderforbundet i Danmark* (General Workers' Union in Denmark; SiD), a major coalition of Danish labor unions, has been especially generous in the 2000s in supporting COSIBAH and COLSIBA with funds obtained from the Danish government. SiD paid for one of COSIBAH's two pickup trucks, for example, and has paid for extensive projects regarding occupational safety and health, as well as COSIBAH salaries.[12] In Honduras, the Irish Catholic development agency Trócaire pays for COSIBAH's radio programs and bought the other pickup.[13] Banana Link, in England, has also funded banana union projects.

These funds flow into COSIBAH and COLSIBA at a general level to the clear benefit of the banana women. They keep both federations in existence, support the all-important struggle with the banana corporations, and sustain the overall organizing, networking, and educational work of the two coalitions. They also subsidize women's projects indirectly, as when rank-and-file workers learn about workshops and conferences over the radio or when Iris regularly drives COSIBAH's truck to Guatemala, Nicaragua, and all over Honduras.

But, as we've seen, the women also get their own independent funding. SiD, the Danish labor federation, in 2001 paid for the COLSIBA women's *Diagnóstico* and in 2003 provided $3,000 to edit and publish their collection of autobiographies.[14] Other grants flow through COSIBAH or COLSIBA at the general level, but are tagged for women's work. In 2002 the AFL-CIO paid for two years of Zoila Lagos's salary to support women's projects in COSIBAH and COLSIBA as part of a package also funding Nelson Nuñez in his work as an organizer, largely in Honduras but also among banana workers in Ecuador. Nelson, in turn, as we've seen, has been crucial in organizing women workers.[15]

In recent years the most generous funds for women's independent projects have come from European NGOs. *Pan Para el Mundo* (Bread for the World), a consortium of German churches, consumer organizations, and support groups for Latin American workers, has paid Iris Munguía's salary since August 2002. In 2003 it funded COSIBAH's sewing, cooking, and other classes for older banana women; in 2004 it paid for the women's all-important computers. Trócaire, similarly, gave FETRABACH's women in Nicaragua $14,000 for their projects in 1999; more recently, it funded the microenterprise project of which the women's pig collective in Honduras is a part.[16]

Of course there are enormous power politics behind all this money, both between funders and fundees, and within the banana unions themselves.[17] In every case outside money shapes the internal gender politics of the banana labor movement, as the women increasingly gain access to independent funding and the organizational autonomy that comes with it. As we've seen, sharp conflicts emerged in earlier years over women's lack of control of money—remember, for example, how in 1984 and 1985 SITRATERCO women were enraged when male leaders failed to share ILO funds earmarked specifically for women's work. We've also seen how, within COLSIBA, at times not all funds assigned to women's work have always ended up in the women's hands—demonstrating the importance of the women's own fiscal control. Since the late 1990s, women's autonomous control of outside funds has made all their flourishing projects possible while legitimating the women's agenda within the banana labor movement as a whole.

Yet they wouldn't have the outside funding in the first place if they didn't also have the institutional rubric of their long-standing, mixed-gender unions, the support of male allies, and their coalitions' own outside support, in turn.

Dynamics of gender and outside funding play themselves out, lastly, in the politics of international travel. The whole transnational network the women have developed depends upon outside money to pay for bus and plane tickets as well as hotel and meeting rooms. International travel has had an enormous impact on both individual banana women and on their collective project as a whole. 'Amanda,' a Guatemalan woman, describes in her autobiography the enormous impact of one single trip:

> I traveled to Costa Rica to participate in a union education event. I lived for two weeks with union comrades that had professional training, and they got me to understand the urgent need to keep studying, not for myself alone, but for all those worker comrades that had chosen me to represent their interests. When I got back to Guatemala I had already made a decision that I wouldn't have changed for anything in the world.[18]

'Amanda' went back to school, as she had promised herself in Costa Rica, and in two years she had a high school diploma and, soon after, a nursing degree.[19] Adela Torres, the sole woman officer in the Colombian banana unions, has been to Costa Rica and Honduras five times. On each trip she has become more central to the banana women's network; on each trip she has grown rapidly in her knowledge of the wider world—especially important for Colombians, since, for safety reasons, outsiders are reluctant to travel to their country.[20]

More than twenty *mujeres bananeras*—from all the countries—have traveled outside of Latin America to the United States or, more often, Europe. Berta Gómez, for example, secretary of women for FETRABACH in Nicaragua, is a tireless, and in many ways exhausted, militant banana activist who has to struggle hard just to keep her family alive. But she benefits from regular travel throughout Central America and once flew to Ireland for free, and she knows eventually she might be invited again to Europe or perhaps to the US.[21] Gloria García, secretary of organization for SITRATERCO, has been not only on six trips within Latin America, but to Washington, DC, Rome, and Finland.[22] 'Carmen,' another SITRATERCO veteran, writes: "Thanks to my union organization I have had the opportunity to know other countries, other cultures, other people, and I have always gotten the most out of it. I've never been handed anything on a silver platter."[23]

Iris Munguía herself has been to Europe several times, in some cases to meet with funders, in others for training workshops, in still others to attend conferences in solidarity with women workers from other sectors. In the banana women's most international moment of all, in July 2000, she attended the first and only global meeting of banana women workers and their allies. Female small producers as well as plantation laborers from Latin America, the Caribbean, Africa, and the Philippines all attended—plus their European allies from the labor movement, consumer groups, and other NGOs. Ironically, the meeting took place not in any banana-producing country, but in Hanover, Germany. That conference captures how crucial Europe is in the banana women's story: in order to simply meet each other, women banana workers traveled not to each others' countries, but to Europe, on European money.[24]

The male leaders within COLSIBA's affiliates are well aware of all this travel and know they can't, largely, control it. They, too, are traveling. They, too, have benefited from the broader horizons, technical advice, and inspiration that travel can offer. Some of the men have traveled not only repeatedly to Denmark, England, France, and on occasion to Washington, DC, but also to the former Soviet Union, Eastern Europe, or the AFL-CIO's US training centers. As the highest-ranking officers of the banana unions in their respective countries, they, too, have independence and access to outside funding. They, too, deal with the complex politics of accepting money from outsiders while trying to maintain autonomy over how that money is spent. What's crucial for our story here is that Northern allies, and the money they choose to spend, have proven a crucial lever in equalizing gender dynamics within the banana unions.

CONCLUSION

Overall, the impact of the banana women's allies has been much greater than the sum of its parts. Any aid, whether facilitation, training, a meager salary, a car, or a trip to Nicaragua or Germany, multiplies by ten within Latin America. For women with no other chance to travel—except perhaps, to visit a grown child in Dallas or Los Angeles—visits to other countries explode their horizons. For women with little more than a sixth-grade education, aid from allies, of many sorts, gives them access to the intellectual resources of those with more advanced educations. For women struggling with sexist leaders of their unions, foreign travel gives them a sense of very different—or often quite similar—gender politics abroad. Perhaps most important, in every case, the women understand the resources they receive to be part of a larger project of empowering other women like themselves at home, and of serving their unions. Think of how 'Amanda' dedicated herself to her education upon her return from her first trip to Costa Rica; or Iris's own first trip to Costa Rica in 1990, from which she came home to teach ten other women in SITRATERCO how to themselves teach ten additional women what she'd learned. Sisterhood, for the *mujeres bananeras* is global, but it's also collective.

Packinghouse worker, Puerto Viejo de Sarapiquí, Heredia, Costa Rica, March 2002.

CONCLUSION

A New Kind of Labor Movement

The women banana workers of Latin America have traveled a long way. Not just from company houses on their plantations in rural Nicaragua or Panamá to meetings in Guayaquil or London across barriers of region and nation, but across enormous barriers of education, generation, and, most important, expectations about their place in the world as women. What began in 1985 in Honduras as a tough fight and a deep collective and personal transformation among women in SITRATERCO expanded in the late 1990s and early 2000s into the flourishing mixed-gender projects of COSIBAH in Honduras, and then the powerful pan–Latin American networks of women in COLSIBA, supported by allies across the world. What began as a local story has become global. That little road trip to Guatemala with which we began now falls into place, I hope, as one remarkable piece of an even more remarkable journey into, and revolution within, the gender politics of the Latin American labor movement.

Bananas are as global an industry as you can get. It's no coincidence that this story emerged in one of the first economic spheres to go fully transnational, way back in the 1890s when United Fruit's tentacular enterprises linked Ecuador with Costa Rica with Boston. In 1993, a century later, new transnational mutations of the banana corporations have similarly compelled the banana unions of Central and South America to think big in new, creative ways, and to construct the national- and regional-level federations in which the women's projects have flourished. Ironically, the very consolidation and crisis of the banana export industry helped open the space for women banana workers' successful activism both in Honduras and throughout Latin America.

Indeed, the transnational nature of the banana industry helps explain, in part, the uniqueness of the banana women's achievements. In many other sectors, Latin American union women and their allies have developed work on a small scale similar to that of the banana workers. Teachers, nurses, maquiladora workers, and other women workers have access to leadership development training, for example.[1] But in none of these sectors have they developed transnational ties among women. Why not? The answer is structural: these other women work for national-level employers, local- or national-level governments, or for fragmented, ephemeral subcontractors difficult to trace to their owners in the North. In the banana export sector, by contrast, unionized women almost all work for the same big three global corporations: Dole, Del Monte, and Chiquita. When COLSIBA in 1993 consolidated banana unions from all three transnational corporations, across seven countries, it created the institutional space for regional women's work. Global banana sisterhood, in other words, has been a subset of labor internationalism.

But it was the banana women themselves who battled their way in to claim and transform that space, and the core elements of their agenda reflect the sophistication with which they have inserted gender politics into COLSIBA and COSIBAH. First, there's the personal: their attention to self-esteem, household dynamics, and their own individual development as leaders. Second, the structural: the sexual division of labor in the home and the broader economy, the politics of sex and gender, and the all-important question of women's packinghouse labor, including not just wages and benefits but job security, housing, reproductive rights, and other issues of occupational health and safety. Third, they have taken on the gender politics of their unions, demanding gender equity in leadership and the validation of women's concerns as central to union politics. Fourth, they have developed into powerful militants in the struggle with the corporations themselves, with a sophisticated understanding of corporate strategy and a deep commitment to advancing all banana workers' rights. Finally, they've turned their eyes to the biggest prize—and the biggest threat facing working-class Latin American men and women: the global economy and its neo-liberal devastation of their communities. The banana women's evolution over time, moreover, recapitulates the women's own development—from individual awakening and empowerment to collective, institutionalized power; from family politics to top-level union politics to the politics of State and global corporate strategy; and from an understanding of the local to a mastery of the national, regional, and the global.

In many ways the banana women's story is an example of the transnational feminisms that emerged in Latin America and world-wide in the 1990s and 2000s.[2] But three problems emerge in iden-tifying the banana women's projects as "transnational feminism." First, as readers may have noticed, the women themselves never use the word "feminism," that is, its Spanish equivalent *feminismo*. Rather, they speak of "women's work," "gender equity," or "gender dynamics." Similarly, the banana women also do not use the word "transnational" (*transnacional*) preferring "regional" (the same word in both English and Spanish) to speak of linkages within Lat-in America. While their new identity as *mujeres bananeras* indeed transcends national boundaries, as do their enterprises, the women also know that their struggles unfold within the context of specific national labor movements, national cultures, and national political dynamics that vary widely.[3] Finally, speaking of their projects as "transnational feminism" alone can suggest the excision of class issues that are so central to the banana women's work. As should be abundantly clear, the banana women never separate their gender politics from their union struggles, and neither should we.[4]

Whatever the terms used to describe their projects, there's no question that women banana workers, along with their male allies, are forging an entirely new definition of what a labor movement looks like. In absolutely unprecedented ways, work on behalf of women's equality and dignity is today understood to be part and parcel of banana unionism in a large swath of Latin America. Ari-ane Grau Crespo, from ASEPROLA, in her introduction to the collection of banana women's autobiographies, sums up beauti-fully the goals of the women's work:

In our opinion, a new way of building unions implies not just the quantitative incorporation of women in all activities, but also learning from them, from their perspective, from their forms of struggle—and taking women's interests, as they have presented them, to be the interests of the organization.[5]

That's it: women's interests are understood by both men and women as the interests of the *entire* organization.

Better yet, listen to how Selfa Sandoval* from Guatemala describes herself at the conclusion of her autobiography:

I am a unionist of the heart, completely dedicated to a cause that because it's so deeply about social justice, compels me to a greater and greater level of commitment.... But above all I am a woman from head to foot; and as a woman I feel a responsibility to continue raising the banner of dignity, of respect, of pride.[6]

Her identity as a woman, in other words, is inseparable from her identity as a militant union activist, and being a banana woman has made it possible for her to define a labor movement that embraces and nourishes both, and that fights for social justice on the barricades of both gender and class.

Grasping the women banana workers' projects leads us, lastly, to a new understanding of international labor solidarity. COLSIBA itself, with its coordination of union activities across seven far-flung nations, is a new kind of enterprise, a new form of democratic self-management from below by workers themselves—in contrast to the ugly history of Cold War AFL-CIO intervention and the bureaucratic, top-down lethargy of long-standing official international federations like the World Federation of Trade Unions (WFTU) or the International Confederation of Free Trade Unions (ICTFU).[7] COLSIBA's women's projects, integrated more deeply into the coalition's larger whole with every passing year, challenge us to envision international labor solidarity with women's issues at the top of the agenda—in order to build a more powerful *workers'* movement across the globe. Rather than imagining solidarity as a gender-neutral enterprise that in practice seemingly inadvertently empowers men only, we need to think about what international

* Though she uses a pseudonym in her autobiography, Selfa Sandoval asked that her real name be used here.

solidarity can look like for women and men both, and learn from the banana workers' model.[8]

The story of women and men banana workers doesn't, of course, end here; it's still in process. The corporations are still out there maneuvering to obliterate the unions; paramilitaries and other armed groups are still out there plotting assassinations and kidnappings; neoliberal governments are still scheming how to impose new trade regimes to crush workers' livelihoods throughout Latin America. But banana unionists are themselves more savvy about global trade politics with every passing year, and their unions are constructing deeper and deeper levels of solidarity at the national, regional, and international levels every day. And together, the banana women and men are still marching forward on the path to gender equality.

We can conclude by handing the story back to the banana women themselves, in their own words. For, if nothing else, the banana women's projects have given them their own voices with which to express their vision of women's dignity and empowerment, and the ability to imagine, meet, and speak directly to allies across the world. Listen, first, to 'Antonia,' a rank-and-file banana woman, in her autobiography:

> I hope that you remember me when it's 12 at night and you think of me even though I don't know you. I hope to know you some day; and I hope that I am granted this wish to know you. This is my greatest wish, to know someone to whom I've confessed what happened in my life.[9]

The last word goes to Iris Munguía, in her introduction to the autobiographies, when she speaks on behalf of all the authors—and, I hope, on behalf of this volume as well:

> We hope that when you read this book it helps you reflect, and that it turns into an incentive for exchange and communication, and for the search for alternative alliances to improve women's lives—not just women in the banana sector, but all women.[10]

Oneyda Galindo, first woman president of a banana workers' union in Latin American history, Buenos Amigos Plantation, El Progreso, Yoro, Honduras, September 2004

Notes

INTRODUCTION

1. This account of the women's trip to Morales is based on personal observation by the author, November 6–7, 2002. Iris Munguía, interviews by the author, November 18, 2002 and September 3, 2003, La Lima, Cortés, Honduras.

2. Selfa Sandoval Carranza, interview by the author, November 7, 2002, Morales, Izabal, Guatemala.

3. "Lessons from SITRABI Victory," *U.S./Labor Education in the Americas Project Newsletter* [hereafter *US/LEAP Newsletter*], April 2001; "Del Monte Leaders Testify Then Go Into Exile," *US/LEAP Newsletter*, April 2002; www.usleap .org; "Labor Dispute Nearing Settlement in Guatemala," *Miami Herald*, March 21, 2000; Sandoval, interview, November 7, 2002; Jesús María Martínez, interview by the author, November 7, 2002, Morales, Izabal, Guatemala; Enrique Villeda, interview by the author, May 12, 2003, Bell Gardens, CA; Sandoval, telephone interview by the author, November 9, 2004.

4. Personal observation by the author. For workshop form and content: "Apuntes Sobre Violencia Doméstica, Jornada sobre Violencia Doméstica; Mujeres Trabajadoras Bananeras COLSIBA SITRABI-UNSITRAGUA, November 2002, Guatemala"; "Programa, Seminario de Educación Sindical, Proyecto Educación COLSIBA-SITRABI, 7 Noviembre Del 2002"; "Jornada Sobre: Violencia Doméstica, Parte Social, Jornada Con Mujeres Trabajadoras Bananeras," [n.d.], all in possession of the author.

5. Maxine Molyneaux, "Mobilization Without Emancipation? Women's Interests, the State, and Revolution in Nicaragua," *Feminist Studies* 11, no. 2 (1985): 227–54; Molyneaux, "Women's Role in the Nicaraguan Revolutionary Process: The Early Years," in *Promissory Notes: Women in the Transition to Socialism*, ed. Sonia Kruks, Rayna Rapp, and Marilyn B. Young, 127–47 (New York: Monthly Review Press, 1989); Molyneaux, *Women's Movements in International Perspective: Latin America and Beyond* (London: Institute of Latin American Studies, 2003); Margaret Randall, *Sandino's Daughters: Testimonies of Nicaraguan Women in Struggle* (Vancouver, BC: New Star Books, 1981); Randall, *Sandino's Daughters Revisited: Feminism*

in Nicaragua (New Brunswick, NJ: Rutgers University Press, 1994); Norma Stoltz Chinchilla, "Revolutionary Popular Feminism in Nicaragua: Ideologies, Political Transitions, and the Struggle for Autonomy," in *Women in the Latin American Development Process,* ed. Christine E. Bose and Edna Acosta-Belén, 242–70 (Philadelphia, PA: Temple University Press, 1995); Karen Kampwirth, *Women and Guerrilla Movements: Nicaragua, El Salvador, Chiapas, Cuba* (University Park: Pennsylvania State University Press, 2002); Julie D. Shayne, *The Revolution Question: Feminisms in El Salvador, Chile, and Cuba* (New Brunswick, NJ: Rutgers University Press, 2004). On the past decade: Lynn Stephen, *Women and Social Movements in Latin America* (Austin, TX: University of Texas Press, 1997), especially 56–107; Jennifer Bickham Méndez, "Creating Alternatives From a Gender Perspective: Transnational Organizing for Maquila Workers' Rights in Central America," in *Women's Activism and Globalization: Linking Local Struggles and Transnational Politics*, ed. Nancy A. Naples and Manisha Desai, 121-41 (New York: Routledge University Press, 2002); Florence Babb, *After Revolution: Mapping Gender and Cultural Politics in Neoliberal Nicaragua* (Austin: University of Texas Press, 2001); Katherine Isbester, *Still Fighting: The Nicaraguan Women's Movement, 1977–2000* (Pittsburgh, PA: University of Pittsburgh Press, 2001).

6. On the *encuentros*: Nancy Saporta Sternbach, Marysa Navarro-Aranguren, Patricia Chuchryk, and Sonia E. Álvarez, "Feminisms in Latin America: From Bogotá to San Bernardo," in *The Making of Social Movements in Latin America*, ed. Sonia E. Álvarez, 207–239 (Boulder, CO: Westview Press, 1992); Sonia E. Álvarez, "Translating the Global: Effects of Transnational Organizing on Local Feminist Discourses and Practices in Latin America," *Meridians: Feminism, Race, Transnationalism* 1, no. 1 (2000): 29–67; Stephen, *Women and Social Movements,* 15–20, 82–83; Marysa Navarro, "First Feminist Meeting of Latin America and the Caribbean," *Signs* 8, no. 1 (1982): 154–57.

7. On the DIGNAS: Stephen, *Women and Social Movements*, 56–107; for women and other social movements: Stephen, *Women and Social Movements*; Marysa Navarro, "The Personal Is Political: Las Madres de Plaza de Mayo," in *Power and Popular Protest: Latin American Social Movements*, ed. Susan Eckstein, 241–58 (Berkeley: University of California Press, 1989).

8. For women and the labor movement in Latin America: Marysa Navarro, "Hidden, Silent, and Anonymous: Women Workers in the Argentine Trade Union Movement," in *The World of Women's Trade Unionism: Comparative Historical Essays*, ed. Norbert C. Soldon, 165–98 (Westport, CT: Greenwood, 1985); John D. French with Mary Lynn Pederson Cluff, "Women and Working-Class Mobilization in Postwar Sao Paulo, 1945–1948," in *The Gendered Worlds of Latin American Women Workers: From Household and Factory to the Union Hall and Ballot Box*, ed. John D. French and Daniel James, 176–207 (Durham, NC: Duke University Press, 1997); Deborah Levenson-Estrada, "The Loneliness of Working-Class Feminism: Women in the 'Male World' of Labor Unions, Guatemala City, 1970s," in *Gendered Worlds*, 208–31; Teresa Carillo, "Women and Independent Unionism in the Garment Industry," in *Popular Movements and Political Change*, eds. Joe Foweraker and Ana L. Craig (Boulder, CO: Lynne Rienner Publications, 1990).

9. On the AFL-CIO and Cold War intervention in Latin American labor: Beth Sims, *Workers of the World Undermined: American Labor's Role in U.S. Foreign Policy* (Boston: South End Press, 1992); Daniel Cantor and Juliet Schor, *Tunnel Vision: Labor, the World Economy and Central America* (Boston: South End Press, 1987); Fred Hirsch and Richard Fletcher, *The CIA and the Labor Movement* (Nottingham, UK: Spokesman, 1977); George Morris, *CIA and American Labor: The Subversion of the AFL-CIO's Foreign Policy* (New York: International Publishers, 1969); Hobart Spalding, Jr., "U.S. and Latin American Labor: The Dynamics of Imperialist Control," in *Ideology and Social Change in Latin America*, eds. June Nash, Juan Corradi, and Hobart Spalding, Jr., 55–91 (New York, NY: Gordon and Breach, 1977); Al Weinrub and William Bollinger, *The AFL-CIO in Latin America: A Look at the American Institute for Free Labor Development (AIFLD)* (Oakland, CA: Labor Network on Central America, 1987); Deb Preusch and Tom Barry, *AIFLD in Central America: Agents as Organizers* (Albuquerque, NM: The Resource Center, 1990).

   For maquiladora organizing: Ralph Armbruster-Sandoval, "Globalization and Cross-Border Labor Organizing: The Guatemala Maquiladora Industry and the Phillips Van Heusen Workers' Movement," *Latin American Perspectives* 26, no. 2 (1999): 108–28; Armbruster-Sandoval, *Globalization and Cross-Border Labor Solidarity in the Americas: The Anti-Sweatshop Movement and the Struggle for Social Justice* (New York: Routledge, 2005); Henry Frundt, "Central American Unions in the Era of Globalization," *Latin American Research Review* 7, no. 3 (Summer 2002); Devon G. Peña, *The Terror of the Machine: Technology, Work, Gender, and Ecology on the U.S.-Mexico Border* (Austin: Center for Mexican American Studies, University of Texas at Austin, 1997); Méndez, "Creating Alternatives"; STITCH (Support Team for Textileras), *Women Behind the Labels: Worker Testimonies from Central America* (Chicago: STITCH and Toronto, ON: Maquiladora Support Network, 2000); Jane L. Collins, *Threads: Gender, Labor, and Power in the Global Apparel Industry* (Chicago: University of Chicago Press, 2003) 177–82; *US/LEAP Newsletter*; Sharon A. Navarro, "Las Voces de Esperanza/ Voices of Hope: La Mujer Obrera, Transnationalism, and NAFTA-Displaced Women Workers in the U.S.-Mexico Boderlands," in *Globalization on the Line: Culture, Capital, and Citizenship at U.S. Borders*, ed. Claudia Sadowski-Smith, 183–200 (New York: Palgrave, 2002); Manuel Rafael Mancíllas, "Transborder Collaboration: The Dynamics of Grassroots Collaboration," in *Globalization on the Line*, 201–220.

10. For a discussion of the problems inherent in the victim model of contemporary support for women maquiladora workers: Dana Frank, "Where Are the Workers in Consumer-Worker Alliances? Class Dynamics and the History of Consumer-Labor Campaigns," *Politics & Society* 31, no. 3 (September 2003) 363–79. Ethel Brooks, "The Ideal Sweatshop: Gender and Transnational Protest," *International Labor and Working-Class History*, no. 61 (Spring 2002): 91–111.

11. Iris Munguía, interview by the author, November 11, 2004, Santa Cruz, California.

CHAPTER ONE

1. For an excellent, crisp introduction to the big picture of contemporary banana export production: Laura T. Raynolds, "The Global Banana Trade," in *Banana Wars: Power, Production, and History in the Americas*, ed. Steve Striffler and Mark Moberg, 23–47 (Durham, NC: Duke University Press, 2003); see also U.S./Labor Education in the Americas Project, *A Strategic Analysis of the Central American Banana Industry: An Industry in Crisis* (Chicago: US/LEAP; Washington, DC: AFL-CIO American Center for International Labor Solidarity, 2000). On the Caribbean: Gordon Myers, *Banana Wars: The Price of Free Trade* (London: Zed Books, 2004).

2. German Zepeda, interview by the author, August 31, 2004, La Lima, Cortés, Honduras.

3. In addition to Raynolds, "Global Banana Trade," for the big picture of the banana export trade, including the long-term shift to subcontracting, see Striffler and Moberg, *Banana Wars*, especially Marcelo Bucheli, "United Fruit Company in Latin America," 80–100; consult, as well, its bibliography on banana production and its history. On subcontracting in Ecuador: Steve Striffler, *In the Shadows of State and Capital: The United Fruit Company, Popular Struggle, and Agrarian Restructuring in Ecuador, 1900–1995* (Durham, NC: Duke University Press, 2002); on structural changes: US/LEAP, *A Strategic Analysis of the Central American Banana Industry*. For up-to-date information on the industry and its labor relations, see *Banana Trade News Bulletin* (Norwich, UK), available online at www.bananalink.org.uk.

4. Human Rights Watch, *Tainted Harvest: Child Labor and Obstacles to Organizing on Ecuador's Banana Plantations* (New York: Human Rights Watch, 2002); Dana Frank, "Our Fruit, Their Labor, and Global Reality," *Washington Post*, June 2, 2002. For export statistics: *Banana Trade News Bulletin*, March 2002, 3; *Banana Trade News Bulletin*, July 2003, 4, 5; *SOPISCO News*, weekly reports on the Latin American banana trade (http://www.sopisco.com/sopisconews/); "Informe Ecuador, Taller de COLSIBA del Secretariado de la Mujer, San Pedro Sula—Honduras, Agosto 27–29, 2003," in possession of the author.

5. On the coup: the classic source is Stephen Schlesinger and Stephen Kinzer, *Bitter Fruit: The American Coup in Guatemala* (Cambridge, MA: Harvard University Press, 1982). On United Fruit, Standard Fruit, and US interests: consult the excellent bibliography and articles in Striffler and Moberg, *Banana Wars*. On the history of banana workers, especially issues of ethnicity and identity: Aviva Chomsky, *West Indian Workers and the United Fruit Company in Costa Rica, 1870–1940* (Baton Rouge: Louisiana State University Press, 1996); Phillippe I. Bourgois, *Ethnicity at Work: Divided Labor on a Central American Banana Plantation* (Baltimore: Johns Hopkins University Press, 1989); Mark Moberg, *Myths of Ethnicity and Nation: Immigration, Work, and Identity in the Belize Banana Industry* (Knoxville: University of Tennessee Press, 1996); Lara Putnam, *The Company They Kept: Migrants and the Politics of Gender in Caribbean Costa Rica, 1870–1960* (Chapel Hill: University of North Carolina Press, 2002).

6. Guatemala: Jim Handy, *Gift of the Devil: A History of Guatemala* (Boston, MA: South End Press, 1984); Susanne Jonas, *The Battle for Guatemala:*

Rebels, Death Squads, and US Power (Boulder, CO: Westview Press, 1991); Jonas, *Of Centaurs and Doves: Guatemala's Peace Process* (Boulder, CO: Westview Press, 2000); Victor Perera, *Unfinished Conquest: The Guatemalan Tragedy* (Berkeley: University of California Press, 1993). Nicaragua: Thomas W. Walker, *Nicaragua: The Land of Sandino* (Boulder, CO: Westview Press, 1986); Walker, *Nicaragua: Living in the Shadow of the Eagle* (Boulder, CO: Westview Press, 2003). El Salvador: Elisabeth Jean Wood, *Insurgent Collective Action and Civil War in El Salvador* (Cambridge and New York: Cambridge University Press, 2003); James Dunkerley, *The Long War: Dictatorship and Revolution in El Salvador* (London: Junction Books, 1982); Marvin E. Gettleman, *El Salvador: Central America in the New Cold War* (New York: Grove Press, 1987).

7. Gilbert Bermúdez Umaña, *El Solidarismo y los Arreglos Directos en las Fincas Bananeras de Costa Rica* (San José, Costa Rica: Leonardo Umaña Vargas / Zeta Servicios Gráficos, 2000); Bermúdez Umaña, interview by the author, San José, Costa Rica, March 27, 2002; Bermúdez Umaña, e-mail message to the author, July 17, 2004.

8. Stephen Coats, telephone interview by the author, July 26, 2004. German Zepeda, interview by the author, May 18, 2005, Oakland, CA. For the best overview of the situation of the banana unions in Central America: US/LEAP, *A Strategic Analysis*; on the banana unions: Henry Frundt, "Central American Unions in the Era of Globalization"; Iris Munguía, interview by the author, November 11, 2004, Santa Cruz, CA.

9. Coats, interview, July 26, 2004; German Zepeda, interview by the author, November 13, 2002, La Lima, Cortés, Honduras. This statistic changes after early 2004, when Chiquita sold off its Colombia holdings.

10. *US/LEAP Newsletter*, December 2001, 8. For a pro-Chiquita account from insiders working with Chiquita: J. Gary Taylor and Patricia J. Scharlin, *Smart Alliance: How a Global Corporation and Environmental Activists Transformed a Tarnished Brand* (New Haven, CT: Yale University Press, 2004); "IUF and Chiquita Agreement on Freedom of Association, Minimum Labor Standards and Employment in the Latin American Banana Sector," June 2001, available at www.usleap.org (in Spanish at www.colsiba.org); "Chiquita: A Strategy That's Bearing Fruit," *Brand Strategy*, May 12, 2003; "SB20 Company Profile: Chiquita Brands International," *Progressive Investor* 1, no. 5, (February 2003); "Importante Acuerdo con CHIQUITA Sobre Libertad Sindical," *Boletín COLSIBA* 4 no. 18 (2001): 11.

11. US/LEAP, *A Strategic Analysis*; sample contracts in the possession of the author: *Contrato Colectivo de Trabajo Celebrado entre La Tela Railroad Company y el Sindicato de Trabajadores de La Tela Railroad Company (SITRATERCO)*, La Lima, Honduras, December 27, 2000, *Pacto Colectivo de Condiciones de Trabajo*, Compañia de Desarollo Bananero de Guatemala, S.A. (Del Monte), and Sindicato de Trabajadores Bananeros De Izabal, Izabal, Guatemala, 2000; Zepeda, interviews, November 13, 2002, and August 31 2004, La Lima, Cortés, Honduras; Coats, interview, July 26, 2004.

12. For the introduction of women into the packinghouses: John Soluri, *Banana Cultures: Production, Consumption, and Eco-social Change in Honduras, 1870–1975* (forthcoming), chap. 6; Munguía, interview, November 18, 2002. For gender dynamics in the Central American banana sector before the

1960s: Lara Putnam, *The Company They Kept.* For the pioneering analysis of gender, women, and the global banana industry: Cynthia Enloe, *Bananas, Beaches, and Bases: Making Feminist Sense of International Politics* (Berkeley: University of California Press, 1990), 124–50.

Just as this book was going to press, a new study of women banana workers in Colombia came out, too late, unfortunately, to include its contents here: Clara Elena Gómez Velásquez, *Derechos y reveses: De las trabajadoras de la agroindustria del banano en Urabá* (Medellín, Colombia: Escuela Nacional Sindical, 2004).

13. Coordinación Regional de la Secretaria de la Mujer, COLSIBA, *Diagnóstico Participativo Con Enfoque de Género Sobre Condiciones Sociales, Economicas, Laborales y Organizativas de las Mujeres Trabajadoras Bananeras* (La Lima, Honduras: COLSIBA, 2001); archives of the *Coordinadora de Sindicatos Bananeros y Agroindustriales* (COSIBAH), COSIBAH office, La Lima, Cortés, Honduras (hereafter COSIBAH Archives); Munguía, interviews, November 18, 2002, and September 3, 2003; personal observation by the author.

14. Domitila Hernández, interview by the author, November 7, 2002, Morales, Izabal, Guatemala.

15. Gloria García, interview by the author, November 5, 2002, La Lima, Cortés, Honduras.

16. *Lo Que Hemos Vivido: Luchas de Mujeres Bananeras* (San José, Costa Rica: Asociación de Servicios de Promoción Laboral, 2003), 124.

17. COLSIBA, *Diagnóstico Participativo*, 20–25; Edilberta Gómez, interview by the author, November 15, 2002, El Viejo, Chinandega, Nicaragua; "Denuncian Muerte de Mujeres por Cancer Contraido por Uso de Nemagon," *Boletín COLSIBA*, 4 no. 18, (2001): 3.

18. COLSIBA, *Diagnóstico Participativo*; contracts, cited above, between SITRATERCO and La Tela Railroad Company (Chiquita), and between SITRABI and Del Monte; Nelson Nuñez, interview by the author, September 2, 2003, La Lima, Cortés, Honduras; *Lo Que Hemos Vivido*; Coordinating Committee of Foro Emaus, *Bananas for the World—And the Negative Consequences for Costa Rica? The Social and Environmental Impacts of the Banana Industry in Costa Rica* (San José, Costa Rica: Foro Emaus, 1998), 35–36, 43; Iris Munguía, interview by the author, August 29, 2004, La Lima, Cortés, Honduras.

19. Edilberta Gómez, interview by the author, August 25, 2004, El Viejo, Chinandega, Nicaragua; Adela Torres, interview by the author, September 2, 2004, Puerto Cortés, Honduras; Carmen Molina, interview by the author, September 2, 2004, Puerto Cortés, Honduras; Edelina García, interview by the author, September 2, 2004, Puerto Cortés, Honduras; Isabel Carraco, interview by the author, September 2, 2004, Puerto Cortés, Honduras; German Zepeda, interview by the author, September 1, 2004, La Lima, Cortés, Honduras.

20. *Lo Que Hemos Vivido*, 138; Miriam Gómez Sánchez, "Acoso Sexual en las Fincas Bananeras," *El Rodín*, January–February 2003, 2 (bulletin of SITRAP, Siquirres, Costa Rica, in possession of the author).

21. *Lo Que Hemos Vivido*, 133; for additional descriptions of the hours of work and the double day: Secretaria de la Mujer, COSIBAH, "Ayuda Memoria

Jornada Sobre Necesidades Prácticas y Necesidades Estratégicas de las Mujeres, Division Sexual de Trabajo,Valle de Aguán y Valle de Sula, 5 de Mayo de 2001," 12–13, COSIBAH Archives.

22. Foro Emaus, *Bananas for the World*, 35.
23. "Resumen Ejecutivo del Proyecto de fortalecimiento de la secretaría de la Mujer de COLSIBA 2002–2004," 3, COSIBAH Archives.
24. COLSIBA, *Diagnóstico Participativo*, 13; Munguía, interview, November 18, 2002.
25. COLSIBA, *Diagnóstico Participativo*, 36.
26. *Lo Que Hemos Vivido*, 104.
27. Domitila Hernández, interview; Munguía, interview, November 18, 2002.
28. Gladys Briones, interview by the author, August 25, 2003, La Lima, Cortés, Honduras.
29. Iris Munguía, interview, September 2, 2003; COLSIBA, *Diagnóstico Participativo*, 32, 39.
30. Munguía, interview, August 29, 2004.
31. COLSIBA, *Diagnóstico Participativo*, 32; Foro Emaus, *Bananas for the World*, 41–54.
32. Foro Emaus, *Bananas for the World*, 36–37, 41–56; Carlos Argüedas Mora, interview by the author, January 19, 2004, Siquirres, Limón, Costa Rica; COLSIBA, *Diagnóstico Participativo*, 32.
33. COLSIBA, *Diagnóstico Participativo*, 11, 13, 26; Munguía, interview, September 3, 2003. For Honduran migration to the United States: Pastoral Social/Cáritas, *Sueños Truncados: La Migración de Hondureños Hacia Estados Unidos* (Tegucigalpa, Honduras: Editorial Guaymuras, 2003).
34. Alcides Hernández, *El Neoliberalismo en Honduras* (Tegucigalpa, Honduras: Editorial Guaymuras, 1983); for the bigger Central American context: William I. Robinson, *Transnational Conflicts: Central America, Social Change, and Globalization* (New York and London: Verso Books, 2003).

CHAPTER TWO

1. Personal observation by the author, November 5, 2002.
2. Mario Argueta, *La Gran Huelga Bananera: Los 69 Días que Estremecieron a Honduras* (Tegucigalpa, Honduras: Editorial Universitaria, 1995); Marvin Barahona, *El Silencio Quedó Atrás: Testimonios de la Huelga Bananera de 1954* (Tegucigalpa, Honduras: Editorial Guaymuras, 1994); Mario Posas, *Lucha Ideológica y Organización Sindical en Honduras (1954–65)* (Tegucigalpa, Honduras: Editorial Guaymuras, 1980); Mario Posas, *Luchas Del Movimiento Obrero Hondureño* (San José, Costa Rica: Editorial Universitaria Centroamericana, 1981); Robert MacCameron, *Bananas, Labor, and Politics in Honduras: 1954–1963* (Syracuse, NY: Maxwell School of Citizenship and Public Affairs, Syracuse University, 1983). For an overview of post-WWII Honduran history through the 1980s, including its labor and peasant movements, and SITRATERCO in particular: James Dunkerley, *Power in the Isthmus: A Political History of Modern Central America* (London and New York: Verso, 1988), 517–81.

3. For SITRATERCO, and its relationship with the AFL-CIO and US State Department, see note above. The best sources for the details of the relationship are in the records of the International Affairs Department and its individual officers, in the AFL-CIO Archives, George Meany Center, Silver Spring, MD, and the records of the US State Department, National Archives II, Silver Spring, MD. For details: Dana Frank, *Imperial Solidarity: U.S. Labor and the Challenge of Internationalism* (New York: The New Press, in progress). For a sampling of AFL-CIO activities in Honduras: see, e.g., American Institute for Free Labor Development, "AIFLD in Honduras: A Success Story," November 15, 1971, record group 18-010, box 6, folder 9, George Meany Archives, AFL-CIO, Silver Spring, MD.

4. A plaque on the front of the building, from 1960, celebrates SITRATERCO's alliance with the ORIT, an AFL-CIO creature. SITRATERCO's 2000 contract with Chiquita's Honduran subsidiary, The Tela Railroad Company, includes the clause 10 F: "Permissions without loss of paid time in order to attend union education programs.

    "The Company, with previous written request on the part of the General Executive Committee, will grant permission without loss of paid time in order to attend courses for union education and training; local, national, and international observation trips; labor seminars and conferences; and for the use of fellowships granted by public or private institutions, national or foreign.

    "This grant will allow a maximum of one thousand eight hundred (1,800) man-hours a year, distributed at the discretion of the union without damage to the services or good advance of the Company."

5. Gloria García, interview by the author, November 5, 2002, La Lima, Cortés, Honduras; Manuel Hernández, interview by the author, November 5, 2002; *Estatuos del Sindicato de Trabajadores de la Tela Railroad Company, SITRATERCO* (La Lima, Cortés, Honduras, [1987]), COSIBAH Archives.

6. Mirian Reyes, interview by the author, August 22, 2003, La Lima, Cortés, Honduras; Zepeda, interview, November 13, 2002; Munguía, interview, November 18, 2002; *Lo Que Hemos Vivido*, 80. For SITRATERCO in the 1970s and early 80s: *Honduras: Historias No Contadas* (Tegucigalpa, Honduras: Centro de Documentación de Honduras [CEDOH], 1985), 81–123; Victor Meza, *Antología de Documentos sobre la Situación y Evolución del Movimiento Obrero en Honduras (1970–1979)* (Tegucigalpa, Honduras: Editorial Universitaria, 1981), 414–20, 549–71.

7. *Lo Que Hemos Vivido*, 80.

8. Manuel Hernández, interview; Munguía, interviews, November 18, 2002 and August 24, 2004; Zepeda, interview, November 13, 2002; *Lo Que Hemos Vivido*, 88; Deborah Levenson found the same pattern, of women as *secretaria de actas*, in the Guatemala City labor movement in the 1980s and 90s (Deborah Levenson-Estrada, "Working-Class Feminism," 24.)

9. *Lo Que Hemos Vivido*, 88.

10. Ibid., 90.

11. Randall, *Sandino's Daughters Revisited*; Babb, *After Revolution*; Molyneaux, "Mobilization Without Emancipation?"; Stephen, *Women and Social Movements in Latin America*; Méndez, "Creating Alternatives."

12. Norma Iris Rodríguez, interview by the author, August 29, 2003, El Progreso, Yoro, Honduras. For women in the Honduran peasant movement in the 1980s: Medea Benjamin, ed., *Don't Be Afraid, Gringo: A Honduran Woman Speaks From the Heart: The Story of Elvia Alvarado* (San Francisco: Institute for Food and Development Policy, 1987).

13. Gloria García, interview by the author, November 18, 2002, La Lima, Cortés, Honduras; *Lo Que Hemos Vivido*, 90.

14. *Lo Que Hemos Vivido*, 90.

15. Ibid., 90.; Munguía, interview, November 18, 2002; Gloria García, interview, November 18, 2002; Reyes, interview.

16. *Lo Que Hemos Vivido*, 90.

17. Gloria García, interview, November 18, 2002.

18. *Lo Que Hemos Vivido*, 91.

19. Ibid., 91; Reyes, interview; Munguía, interview, November 18, 2002; Gloria García, interview, November 18, 2002.

20. Gloria García, interview, November 18, 2002.

21. *Lo Que Hemos Vivido*, 92; Reyes, interview; Munguía, interviews, November 18, 2002 and August 29, 2004.

22. *Hablemos de la Diferencia, Mujer y Sociedad, Mujer y Trabajo, Liderazgo*, booklets from Proyecto OIT/DANIDA para Mujeres Trabajadoras Rurales, n.d., COSIBAH Archives.

23. *Lo Que Hemos Vivido*, 104.

24. Ibid., 92. Reyes, interview; Munguía, interview, November 18, 2002. For more on this model for education: *Lo Que Hemos Vivido*; it was expounded at all the workshops I myself observed in 2002.

25. Munguía, interview, August 29, 2004.

26. *Lo Que Hemos Vivido*, 92.

27. Ibid., 103.

28. Ibid., 104; Reyes, interview; Munguía, interview, November 18, 2002; *Lo Que Hemos Vivido*, 92, 103–04.

29. *Lo Que Hemos Vivido*, 88.

30. Munguía, interview, November 18, 2002.

31. Reyes, interview.

32. *Lo Que Hemos Vivido*, 84.

33. Ibid., 95.

34. E.g. Ibid., 83, 102.

35. Ibid., 93.

36. Ibid., 93.

37. Gloria García, interview, November 18, 2002.

38. Bermúdez Urmaña, *El Solidarismo*; José María Martínez, interview, August 26, 2004, La Lima, Cortés, Honduras.

39. *Lo Que Hemos Vivido*, 93, 84, 108.

40. Ibid., 104–119.

41. Ibid., 96.

42. Ibid., 84.

43. Ibid., 105.

44. Reyes, interview; Munguía, interviews, November 18, 2002 and August 26, 2004, La Lima, Cortés, Honduras. The first women on the executive

committee were Gladys Valle, 1982–86, Ramona Aguilar, 1986–90, Mirian Reyes, 1990–94, and Iris Munguía, 1994–98.

45. *Lo Que Hemos Vivido*, 96.

46. Ibid., 108; Gloria García, interview, November 5, 2002; Munguía, interview, November 18, 2002.

47. "Natural Disasters and Their Impact on the Region," *ECLAC Notes*, March 1999, 1, 3; US/LEAP, *A Strategic Analysis*, 11–13, 153–57, 160–66; Reyes, interview; Munguía, interview, November 18, 2002; *Lo Que Hemos Vivido*, 74, 76, 81, 100, 111–12; Specialarbejderforbundet i Danmark, "Bananarbejdere i Mellemanerika, SiD's Internationale Kalender 2001: Trabajadores y Trabajadoras Bananeros de Centroamerica," in possession of the author, including "Livet efter MITCH/La Vida Después del MITCH" (October) and "Jeg mistede alti i orkanen MITCH!/Perdí todo con el Huracán Mitch" (November).

48. US/LEAP, *A Strategic Analysis*, 164–65; José María Martínez, interview by the author, November 4, 2002, La Lima, Cortés, Honduras; Zepeda, interview, November 13, 2002; Munguía, interview, November 18, 2002; SiD calendar; "Memoria, Primer Taller Sobre Métodos y Técnicas de la Educación Popular, Proceso de Formación de Educadores de la Coordinadora de Sindicatos Bananeros de Honduras," San Pedro Sula, November 10, 1999, 16, COSIBAH Archives.

49. Gloria García, interview by the author, September 3, 2004, Puerto Cortés, Honduras.

50. Comité Central de Asuntos Femeninos, SITRATERCO, "Informe, 2002," SITRATERCO Archives, SITRATERCO Office, La Lima, Cortés, Honduras; Munguía, interview, November 18, 2002; José María Martínez, interview; "Informe del Comité Central de Asuntos Femeninos del 'SITRATERCO,' A Presentarse Ante La 'V Asamblea General de Mujeres,' A Celebrarse en la Ciudad de La Lima, Depto. de Cortes, El 18 de Diciembre de 1999," COSIBAH Archives.

51. Comité Central de Asuntos Femeninos, SITRATERCO, "Informe 2002."

52. Gloria García, interview, November 18, 2002.

53. Ibid.; Munguía, interview, November 18, 2002.

54. Munguía, "Luchas y Logros de las Mujeres Sindicalistas Bananeras, Septiembre 2004," in possession of the author; personal observation by the author, August 28, 2004.

55. Ibid.

56. Photograph by the author, SITRATERCO negotiating committee members, November 9, 2002, La Lima, Cortés, Honduras.

CHAPTER THREE

1. Personal observation by the author, August 22, 2003, La Lima, Cortés, Honduras; Coordinación del Trabajo de la Mujer COLSIBA, *Conozcamos de Género* (La Lima, Cortés, Honduras, n.d.), COSIBAH Archives.

2. US/LEAP, *A Strategic Analysis of the Central American Banana Industry*, 3–5, 11–19, 31–46; Zepeda, interview, November 13, 2002; Robert Perillo, "Banana Workers and Transnationals: An Industry in Crisis," *US/LEAP*

Newsletter, August 2001; "Banana Industry Crisis Continues to Hit Workers," *US/LEAP Newsletter*, August 2000.

3. Zepeda, interview, August 31, 2004.

4. Zepeda, interview, November 13, 2002; Munguía, interview, November 18, 2002.

5. Munguía, interview, November 18, 2002; Zepeda, interview, November 13, 2002.

6. Munguía, interviews, November 18, 2002 and September 2, 2003.

7. Munguía, interview, November 18, 2002; Reyes, interview; Gloria García, interview, November 18, 2002.

8. Personal observation by the author, August 20, 2003, COSIBAH office, La Lima, Cortés, Honduras.

9. Munguía, interview, November 18, 2002.

10. Munguía, interview, September 3, 2004.

11. "Ayuda Memoria, Primera Conferencia Nacional de Mujeres Bananeras, Coordinadora de Sindicatos Bananeros y Agroindustriales de Honduras," August 15–16, 1996, San Pedro Sula, Honduras, COSIBAH Archives; "Mujeres Demandan Mayor Participación en Sindicatos," *Nueva Visión Sindical*, January 2002, 12–13; Munguía, interview, September 3, 2004.

12. Munguía, interview, September 3, 2004.

13. "Informe, Periodo Junio 98 Hasta Junio 2000, Secretaria de la Mujer COSIBAH," COSIBAH Archives; "Informe Coordinacíon del Trabajo de la Mujer de la Coordinadora de Sindicatos Bananeros y Agroindustriales de Honduras (COSIBAH) Ante la V Asamblea Ordinaria, Periodo de Octobre 2003 a Julio 2003," COSIBAH Archives; "Secretaria de La Mujer COSIBAH Taller Sobre Liderazgo Democrático y Desintegración Familiar, 7 y 8 de Marzo del 2002," COSIBAH Archives; Munguía, interview, September 3, 2003; Secretaria de la Mujer, COSIBAH, *Coordinación del Trabajo de la Mujer Bananera en Honduras* (La Lima, Honduras, n.d. [2002]), pamphlet in possession of the author; also in COSIBAH Archives.

14. Domitila Hernández, *Historia de Vida*, La Lima, Cortés, Honduras, December 2000, 8, COSIBAH Archives. (This autobiography was not included in the final version of *Lo Que Hemos Vivido*).

15. Personal observation by the author, November 15, 2002, El Viejo, Chinandega, Nicaragua; November 7, 2002, Morales, Izabal, Guatemala; Zoila Lagos and Iris Munguía, conversations with the author, August 2002, La Lima, Cortés, Honduras.

16. Iris Munguía and Nicaraguan banana women activists, conversations with the author, Leon, Nicaragua, November 16, 2002; anonymous banana woman activist, interview by the author, November 2002. Jennifer Bickham Méndez observed the use of the same game among women maquiladora activists in the Central American Network of Women in Solidarity with Maquila Workers, at a workshop in the late 1990s, evidently in Nicaragua or El Salvador. Méndez, "Creating Alternatives," 121.

17. Secretaria de la Mujer, COSIBAH, "Ayuda Memoria Jornada"; Zoila Lagos, telephone interview by the author, October 22, 2004.

18. Secretaria de la Mujer, COSIBAH, "Ayuda Memoria Jornada," 1.

19. Ibid., 2.

20. Ibid., 2–8.

21. Ibid., 8–9; Lagos, interview, October 22, 2004.
22. Secretaria de la Mujer, COSIBAH, "Ayuda Memoria Jornada," 9–10; Lagos, interview, October 22, 2004.
23. Zoila Lagos, interview, October 22, 2004.
24. Secretaria de la Mujer, COSIBAH, "Ayuda Memoria Jornada," 12.
25. Ibid., 12–14; Lagos, interview, October 22, 2004.
26. Secretaria de la Mujer, COSIBAH, "Ayuda Memoria Jornada," 14–16.
27. Ibid., 16–17.
28. Munguía, interview, November 18, 2003; SiD calendar; Secretaria de la Mujer, COSIBAH, *Coordinación del Trabajo*; Secretaria de la Mujer COSIBAH, "Informe Periodo Junio 98 Hasta Junio 2000."
29. "Actividades Proyecto COSIBAH, Enero 1999 a Enero 2002," COSIBAH Archives; Secetaria de la Mujer, COSIBAH, *Coordinación del Trabajo*; "COSIBAH y ASEPROLA: Fortaleciendo la Educación en la Region," *Nuevo Visión Sindical*, April 2002, 15; "Informe Coordinacíon del Trabajo."
30. Secretaria de la Mujer, COSIBAH, "Manual Sobre Autoestima," n.d., COSIBAH Archives.
31. Ibid.
32. Ibid.
33. Ibid.
34. Ibid.
35. Ibid.
36. "Segundo Taller del Proceso de Seguimiento en Formación de Cuadros Programa de la Mujer COSIBAH, 1 y 2 de Agosto 2003" and accompanying documents, COSIBAH Archives.
37. "Actividades Proyecto COSIBAH, Enero 1999 a Enero 2002," COSIBAH Archives; Secetaria de la Mujer, COSIBAH, *Coordinación del Trabajo*; "COSIBAH y ASEPROLA," 15; "Informe Coordinacíon del Trabajo"; COSIBAH, "Informe, 2000–2002," COSIBAH Archives; "Talento Femenino," *Nueva Vision Sindical*, January 2002, 4–5; "Programa Formación de Facilidador Coordinación Trabajo de la Mujer COSIBAH, En la Educación Permanente las Mujeres Bananeras Presente, Junio 2003–2004," COSIBAH Archives; "Segundo Taller del Proceso de Seguimiento en Formación de Cuadros Programa de la Mujer COSIBAH, 1 y 2 de Agosto 2003, Tema: Practica de Aplicación de Metodología Popular," COSIBAH Archives. For an example of workshop themes, "¿Qué Es el Autoestima?" *Nueva Visión Sindical*, January 2002, 19.
38. Munguía, interview, November 18, 2002.
39. Lagos, interview, November 12, 2002, La Lima, Cortes, Honduras; Zoila Lagos, "Memorias Zoila Lagos, Primer Tomo," (2000), in possession of the author.
40. Lagos, interview, November 12, 2002.
41. Ibid.
42. Munguía, interview, September 1, 2003, La Lima, Cortés, Honduras; personal observation by the author, August 25, 2003, La Lima, Cortés, Honduras.
43. Munguía, interview, September 1, 2003; Norma Rodríguez, interview; personal observation by the author, August 21, 2003.
44. Nelson Nuñez, interview, September 2, 2003.
45. Liz O'Connor, telephone interview by the author, March 12, 2003.

46. Nuñez, interview.
47. Oneyda Galindo, interview by the author, November 13, 2002, La Lima, Cortés, Honduras; "Nuevo Sindicato Bananero," *Nueva Visión Sindical,* November 2003, 5.
48. José María Martínez, interview; visit by the author to Radio Progreso/ Sindicalista del Aire, August 22, 2003, El Progreso, Yoro, Honduras.
49. *Nueva Visión Sindical,* April 2002.
50. Personal observation by the author, August 22, 2002, La Lima, Cortés, Honduras.
51. Zepeda, interviews, November 13, 2002 and August 31, 2004.
52. Ibid.
53. Alison Acker, *Honduras: The Making of a Banana Republic* (Boston: South End Press, 1988); Richard Lapper and James Painter, *Honduras: State for Sale* (London: Latin America Bureau, 1985); Nancy Peckenham and Annie Street, *Honduras: Portrait of a Captive Nation* (New York: Praeger, 1985); Americas Watch, *Human Rights in Honduras: Central America's "Sideshow"* (New York: Americas Watch, 1987); Centro de Documentación de Honduras y Universidad Internacional de La Florida, *Honduras: Realidad Nacional y Crisis Regional* (Tegucigalpa, Honduras: Centro de Documentación de Honduras, 1986).

CHAPTER FOUR

1. Secretaria de la Mujer, COLSIBA, "Taller Intercambio de Metologías de Trabajo con Perspectiva de Género para Integrar de los Contratos Colectivos de Trabajo," September 1, 2004; Asociación Servicios de Promoción Laboral, "Taller Sobre Metología de Trabajo Con Perspectiva de Género Para Integrar en Los Contratos Colectivos de Trabajo," September 1–2, 2004; "Listado de Participantes," all in possession of the author; personal observation by the author, Puerto Cortés, Cortés, Honduras, September 1–4, 2004.
2. Telma Gómez, conversation with the author, September 4, 2004, La Lima, Cortés, Honduras.
3. Zepeda, interview, November 13, 2002.
4. Zepeda, interviews, November 13, 2002, and August 29, 2004; for background and regular information on COLSIBA, see www.colsiba.org; *US/LEAP Newsletter, Banana Trade News Bulletin; Boletín COLSIBA* 4, no. 18 (2001).
5. "IUF and Chiquita Agreement on Freedom of Association, Minimum Labor Standards and Employment in the Latin American Banana Sector"; Zepeda, interview, November 13, 2002; US/LEAP, *A Strategic Analysis; US/LEAP Newsletter,* June 2001; "Importante Acuerdo con CHIQUITA Sobre Libertad Sindical," *Boletín COLSIBA* 4, no. 18 (2001): 12.
6. Eight thousand belong to unions affiliated with COSIBAH; another 2,000 belong to SUTRASFCO, which represents Dole workers in the Aguán Valley. It was affiliated with COSIBAH at the federation's founding but later left.
7. COLSIBA, www.colsiba.org, August 2, 2003; US/LEAP, *A Strategic Analysis of the Central American Banana Industry,* 73.

8. Edilberta Gómez, interview, November 15, 2002; Edilberta Gómez, interview by the author, September 30, 2004, Puerto Cortés, Honduras; Stephen Coats, telephone interview with the author, August 3, 2004; anonymous women banana activists, conversations with the author, 2002, 2003, and 2004; COLSIBA, *Diagnóstico Participativo*; "Doris Zulema García C.," *COLSIBA*, Año 1, Edición 1 (Julio/Agosto 2004): 14.

9. COLSIBA, www.colsiba.org, August 3, 2004.

10. Irene Barrientos, interview by the author, November 8, 2002, Puerto Barrios, Izabal, Guatemala.

11. Ibid.; www.colsiba.org; US/LEAP, *A Strategic Analysis*, 73; Sandoval, interview, November 7, 2002.

12. Bermúdez Umaña, communication with the author, July 17, 2004; US/LEAP, *A Strategic Analysis*, 95–96; "Capacitación de las Mujeres en SITRAP," *El Rodín* (Sindicato de Trabajadores de Plantaciones Agricolas), November–December 2002, 7; Sánchez, "Acoso Sexual en las Fincas Bananeras"; "Informe de Trabajo Realizado por Comité Femenino de Sindicatos Bananeros de Costa Rica, Periodo: Diciembre 1995," San José, Costa Rica, COLSIBA, COSIBAH Archives.

13. Inés Binns, Ernelda Peterson, and Ayala C. Hilda, Secretaria de la Mujer, Sindicato de Trabajadores de la Industria Bananeras (SITRAIBANA), "Informe del Contexto del Area de Bocas del Toro, República de Panamá, Diagnóstico Participativo con el Enfoque de Género, Sobre las Condiciones Laborales y Socio-Economicas de las Mujeres Bananeras," April 23, 2001, COSIBAH Archives; anonymous, interview by the author, November 18, 2002; Trabajo de la Mujer, COLSIBA, "Situación Socio Economica y Laboral de Las Mujeres Trabajadoras Bananeras en la Region," text of PowerPoint presentation, 2003, 3, in possession of the author.

14. Adela Torres, interview by the author, El Progreso, Yoro, Honduras, August 31, 2003; Adela Torres, interview by the author, Puerto Cortés, Honduras, September 4, 2004; Guillermo Rivera, interview by the author, San José, Costa Rica, January 25, 2004; *US/LEAP Newsletter*, "Chiquita Sells Off Colombian Operations," July 2004; Robert Perillo, "Colombian Trade Unions Under Fire," Special Report, Second Edition, *US/LEAP Newsletter*, January 2004; Juan Forero, "Union Workers in Colombia Are Easy Prey for Gunmen," *New York Times*, April 29, 2001; Juan Forero, "Assassination an Issue in Trade Talks," *New York Times*, November 18, 2004; "Informe Ecuador"; "Adela Torres Baloy," *Boletín COLSIBA* 1, no. 1 (July/August 2004): 15; Escuela Nacional Sindical, Medellín, Colombia, "Programación Campaña Derechos Laborales Sexuales y Reproductivos de las Trabajadoras Bananeras," August 2004, in possession of the author. For an extended discussion of women banana workers in Colombia that was published too late to include its contents here, see Clara Elena Gómez Velásquez, *Derechos y reveses: De las trabajadoras de la agroindustria del banano* (Medellín, Colombia: Escuela Nacional Sindical, 2004).

15. Human Rights Watch, *Tainted Harvest*; Dana Frank, "Our Fruit, Their Labor, and Global Reality," *Washington Post*, June 2, 2002; Max Krochmal, "Sculpting Transnational Unionism: Building a Democratic Labor Movement in Ecuador's Banana Fields" (senior thesis, Community Studies Department, University of California, Santa Cruz, 2004), 120–21, 163–64; Federación

Nacional de Campesinos e Indígenas Libres Del Ecuador, *Por la Organización de los Trabajadores Bananeros del Ecuador*, pamphlet, Guayaquil, Ecuador, n.d., in possession of the author.

16. COSIBAH, "Ayuda Memoria, Análisis de las Acuerdos de la III Conferencia Latinoamericana de Sindicatos Bananeros, En el Ámbito de Los Derechos de las Trabajadoras Bananeras," November 15–16, 1995, Managua, Nicaragua, COSIBAH Archives.

17. Munguía, interviews, November 18, 2002, and September 3, 2003; Iris Munguía, interview by the author, September 1, 2004, La Lima, Cortés, Honduras; Doris Garciá, interview by the author, August 23, 2004, El Viejo, Chinandega, Nicaragua; Edilberta Gómez, interview by the author, August 23, 2004, El Viejo, Chinandega, Nicaragua; Mathilde Aguilar Quiroz, interview by the author, August 23, 2004, El Viejo, Chinandega, Nicaragua.

18. Munguía, interview, November 18, 2002.

19. Iris Yolanda Munguía, "Informe, Secretaria de la Mujer, Coordinadora Latinoamericana de Sindicatos Bananeros," La Lima, Honduras, November 13, 1995, COSIBAH Archives.

20. COSIBAH, "Ayuda Memoria, Análisis de los Acuerdos."

21. "Informe de Trabajo Realizado por la Secretaria de la Mujer, V Conferencia Latinoamerica de Sindicatos Bananeros," Managua, Nicaragua, June 15–18, 1999; "Memoria, Taller Sobre Salud Ocupacional, Coordinadora Latinoamericana de Sindicatos Bananeros," March 17–20, 1998, San Pedro Sula, Cortés, Honduras; both in COSIBAH Archives.

22. 2002 COLSIBA poster in possession of the author; COLSIBA, "Ayuda Memoria, Encuentro Regional de Mujeres Bananeras," August 29–31, 2002, San Pedro Sula, Cortés, Honduras, COSIBAH Archives; "VII Encuentro Latinoamericano de Mujeres Bananeras," *Nueva Visión Sindical*, November 2003, 14–15. For some of the first framing of COLSIBA women's work in terms of the global economy: Coordinación Trabajo de la Mujer, "Informe Del Trabajo de la Mujer COLSIBA," VI Conferencia, Apartado, Colombia, August 8–11, 2001, 1, COSIBAH Archives.

23. "Programa, Seminario Taller, Técnicas y Estrátegias de la Negociación Colectiva, Coordinadora Latinoamericana de Sindicatos Bananeros COLSIBA, Coordinación del Trabajo de la Mujer COLSIBA-COSIBAH," August 27–30, 2003, El Progreso, Yoro, Honduras, COSIBAH Archives; COLSIBA women's conference on collective bargaining, personal observation by the author, August 27–30, 2003, El Progreso, Yoro, Honduras. For COLSIBA women's activities, see also www.colsiba.org/mujertrabajadora. html.

24. COLSIBA, "Ayuda Memoria, Encuentro Regional de Mujeres Bananeras."

25. Ibid.

26. "El VII Encuentro Latinoamericano de Mujeres Bananeras Frente a las Estratégias de Apertura Comercial: ALCA, TLC's y el Plan Puebla Panamá," COSIBAH Archives.

27. COLSIBA women's conferences, observation by the author, August 26–30, 2003, El Progreso, Yoro, Honduras, and January 21–24, 2004, San José, Costa Rica.

28. Sandoval, interview, November 7, 2002; Selfa Sandoval, interview by the author, August 28, 2003, El Progreso, Yoro, Honduras; Iris Munguía,

interview, September 3, 2003; "Selfa Sandoval Carranza," *Boletín COLSIBA* 1, no. 1 (July–August 2004): 17.

29. Personal observation by the author, November 8, 2002, Puerto Barrios, Izabal, Guatemala, and November 7, 2002, Morales, Izabal, Guatemala.
30. Catalina Pérez Querra, interview by the author, November 8, 2002, Puerto Barrios, Izabal, Guatemala.
31. SITRABI, "Proyecto de Educación Para Mujeres Por Condiciones Sociales Justas," n.d., COSIBAH Archives; Selfa Sandoval Carranza, Secretaria de Organización, Prensa y Propaganda, SITRABI, "Informe de Trabajo, Diciembre 2003–Abril 2004," 2, COSIBAH Archives; *El Bananero* (Sindicato Industrial de Trabajadores Agrícolas y Anexos de Heredia), July 2004, 3, in possession of the author; Escuela Nacional Sindical, Medellín, Colombia, "Programación Campaña."
32. COLSIBA, *Diagnóstico Participativo*.
33. Ibid., 5.
34. Ibid.; COLSIBA, "Informe Final Del Taller, Taller de Sistematización de Conclusiones y Recomendaciones, a Partir de los Informes Nacionales del DPEG Sobre Condiciones Sobre-Económicas y Laborales de las Mujeres Bananeras," Honduras, June 29–30, 2001, COSIBAH Archives.
35. COLSIBA, "Informe Final Del Taller," 6–7.
36. COLSIBA, *Diagnóstico Participativo*, 73.
37. See also, Clara Elena Gómez Velásquez, *Derechos y reveses*.
38. Ana Naranjo Porras, *Mujeres Trabajadoras Bananeras: Desafíos y Esperanzas* (San José, Costa Rica: Varitec, 2002); COLSIBA, *Agenda Regional de Las Mujeres Bananeras* (San José, Costa Rica: COLSIBA, 2002).
39. *Lo Que Hemos Vivido*.
40. "Informe Narrativo Concurso, 'Historias de Vida de Mujeres Bananeras en Centroamerica,'" n.d., COSIBAH Archives.
41. Munguía, interview, November 18, 2002.
42. *Lo Que Hemos Vivido*, 13.
43. Munguía, interviews, November 18, 2002, and September 1, 2004.
44. *Lo Que Hemos Vivido*, 9.
45. Ibid.
46. In addition to the books, reports, and pamphlets already noted, COLSIBA in 2004 produced two educational manuals: *Conozcamos de Contractión Colectiva* and a reprint of Pilar Gonzáles Vásquez, *Liderazgos, Lideres y Liderezas: Una Perspectiva de Género Para Organizaciones Laborales de Latinoamerica* (La Lima, Honduras: COLSIBA, 2004); mug in possession of the author.
47. Personal observation by the author, El Viejo and Chinandega, Nicaragua, November 15, 2002.
48. Munguía, interview, November 18, 2003; COLSIBA meetings, observation by the author, Guatemala City, Guatemala, December 14–15, 2000; San José, Costa Rica, March 25, 2002; Chinandega, Nicaragua, November 15–16, 2002; and San José, Costa Rica, January 22–24, 2004.
49. Anonymous interview with the author, November 2002; Iris Munguía noted similarly: "The men are still afraid of a woman officer's leadership. The men don't want to turn over power." (Munguía, interview, September 1, 2004).
50. COSIBAH, "Ayuda Memoria, Análisis de los Acuerdos," 2.

51. Edilberta Gómez, conversation with the author, November 15, 2003, El Viejo, Chinandega, Nicaragua.
52. Munguía, interview, November 18, 2002.
53. COLSIBA, "Informe, Secretaria de la Mujer, Coordinadora Latinoamericana de Sindicatos Bananeros," La Lima, Cortés, Honduras, November 13, 1995, 6, COSIBAH Archives.
54. Munguía, interview, September 3, 2003.
55. "Selfa Sandoval Carranza," *Boletín COLSIBA*, 17.
56. Personal observation by the author, San José, Costa Rica, January 23–24, 2004.
57. Munguía, interview, September 3, 2003.
58. Anonymous woman banana union activist, interview by the author, 2002.
59. For dynamics of gender, the labor movement, and information politics in maquiladora organizing in Central America: Méndez, "Creating Alternatives from a Gender Perspective," 73; in the Guatemalan labor movement, Levenson-Estrada, "Working-Class Feminism," 224.
60. See chapter six for a discussion of this topic.
61. Personal observation by the author, August 30–31, El Progreso, Yoro, Honduras; Munguía, interview by the author, August 31, 2003, El Progreso, Yoro, Honduras. For exact sources of funding, see chapter six, "Global Allies."
62. COLSIBA, "Taller de Sistematización de Conclusiones," 15; Personal observation by the author, El Progreso, Yoro, Honduras, August 28–31, 2003; San José, Costa Rica, January 21–23, 2004; and Puerto Cortés, Cortés, Honduras, September 1–4, 2004; Coordinación Trabajo de la Mujer, "Informe del Trabajo," 5.

CHAPTER FIVE

1. Secretaria de la Mujer, SITRAIBANA, "Informe del Contexto," 1.
2. Reyes, interview.
3. COLSIBA, *Diagnóstico Participativo*, 63; for women making the same report from Guatemala, 63.
4. Ibid., 64.
5. Ibid., 63.
6. Galindo, interview.
7. *Lo Que Hemos Vivido*, 73.
8. Secretaria de la Mujer, COSIBAH, "Ayuda Memoria Jornada," 8.
9. Iris Munguía, conversation with the author, August 2002.
10. Santos Licona, interview by the author, November 13, 2002, La Lima, Cortés, Honduras.
11. Edilberta Gómez, interview, November 15, 2002.
12. Observation by the author, August 24, 2004, El Viejo, Chinandega, Nicaragua.
13. *Lo Que Hemos Vivido*, 94.
14. Deborah Levenson-Estrada found the same patterns in the Guatemala City labor movement during the 1970s and 80s. Male trade unionists "rarely permitted their own wives to become involved in unions," while "most women

trade unionists were not wives." One woman told her: "It is impossible to be a woman trade unionist and be married." Levenson-Estrada, "Working-Class Feminism" (224–25). Another woman activist explained: "But you know the reason I told you this tale is to explain *how* I could get involved in the union. There was no one at home to stop me…no husband, mother, father, mother-in-law, father-in-law. I was alone"(209).

15. Secretaria de la Mujer, COSIBAH, "Ayuda Memoria Jornada," 8.
16. Women banana union activists, conversations with the author, November 2002, August 2003, and September 2003.
17. Secretaria de la Mujer, COSIBAH, "Ayuda Memoria Jornada," 1.
18. *Lo Que Hemos Vivido*, 83.
19. Ibid., 114.
20. Edilberta Gómez, interview, November 15, 2002.
21. Reyes, interview.
22. COLSIBA, *Diagnóstico Participativo*, 71.
23. Lagos, interview, November 12, 2002.
24. 'Marta Rodríguez' (pseudonym), interview with author, 2003.

CHAPTER SIX

1. Lagos, interview, November 12, 2002; Munguía, interviews, November 18, 2002, and September 3, 2003; Norma Iris Rodríguez, interview; anonymous interview by the author, August 2003, La Lima, Cortés, Honduras; pamphlets, Centro de Derechos de Mujeres (CDM), San Pedro Sula, Honduras [2003]: *Hagamos Uso de la Ley Contra la Violencia Doméstica*; *Antes el Cierre de las Fábricas Exige Respecto a Tus Derechos como Trabajadora*; *Cuando Estoy Embarazada, Tengo Derechos, Exijo Respeto*; *Cuando Me Acosan Sexualmente*; *Cuando el Trabajo Afecta Mi Salud*; *Cuando Me Despiden Injustamente*; Comité Regional Femenino COCENTRA, Elaborado por Alba Palacios, *Mujer y Organización Sindical*, [n.d.]; *Lo Que Hemos Vivido*, 76, 100, 115–16; SiD Calendar; *Unidas: Revista Centroamericana*, May 2002, publication of Comité Femenino COCENTRA, in possession of the author; Comité Femenino, COCENTRA Honduras, "Informe de Evaluación, Proyecto 'Desarrollo Sindical para Mujeres de Centroamérica Fase II,'" Tegucigalpa, Honduras, July 2002, COSIBAH Archives; "Educación: También a las Compañeras de las Empacadoras," *Tribuna Sindical* (SUTRASFCO—Sindicato Unificado de Trabajadores de la Standard Fruit Company), segunda época, no. 1: 3, in possession of the author.
2. www. aseprola.org, May 31, 2004; COLSIBA, *Diagnóstico Participativo*, 10; *Lo Que Hemos Vivido*, 7; personal observation by the author, January 21–24, 2004, San José, Costa Rica, and August 28–31, El Progreso, Yoro, Honduras; Munguía, interview, November 18, 2002; Lagos, interview, November 12, 2002; "Ayuda Memoria, Primera Conferencia Nacional de Mujeres Bananeras"; "COSIBAH y ASEPROLA: Fortaleciendo la Educación en la Region"; "Las Implicaciones de un Convenio," (ASEPROLA-COSIBAH), *Nueva Visión Sindical*, January 2002, 6–7; Ana Victoria Naranjo Porras, *Diagnóstico sobre Participación Sindical de la Mujer en Centroamérica* (San José, Costa Rica: ASEPROLA, 2000); ASEPROLA, *Investigación Capacitación*

Asesoría y Comunición para el mundo laboral centroamericano, pamphlet, n.d., in possession of the author.

3. Munguía, interview, September 3, 2003; Lagos, interview, November 12, 2002. On the *encuentros*: see p. 104, n. 6.

4. Munguía, interview, September 3, 2003; poster in possession of the author.

5. COLSIBA, *Conozcamos de Género*; quote, 2. For gender analysis in COSIBAH: "¿Qué Es Eso el Género?" *Nueva Visión Sindical*, April 2002, 18–19.

6. For European banana activism: *Banana Trade News Bulletin*, www.bananalink. org.uk.

7. *US/LEAP Newsletter*; www.usleap.org; "Delegación Estadounidense Analiza Derechos Laborales en Sector Bananero," *El Telégrafo* (Guayaquil, Ecuador), June 1, 2002. US/LEAP's use of political pressure in the US in order to promote labor rights in Latin America fits Margeret Keck and Kathryn Sikkink's "boomerang" model for transnational activism; see Keck and Sikkink, *Activists Beyond Borders: Transnational Advocacy Networks in International Politics* (Ithaca, NY: Cornell University Press, 1998).

8. For an overview, Tim Shorrock, "Labor's Cold War: Freshly Unearthed Documents May Force the AFL-CIO to Face up to Past Betrayals," *Nation* May 19, 2003.

9. Tim Shorrock, "Labor's Cold War"; For a sampling of the debate on Venezuela: Stanley Gacek, "Lula and Chavez: Differing Responses to the Washington Consensus," *New Labor Forum* 13, no. 1 (Spring 2004): 41–49; Robert Collier, "Old Relationships Die Hard: A Response to Stanley Gacek's Defense of the AFL-CIO's Position on Venezuela," and Gacek, "Stanley Gacek Replies," *New Labor Forum* 13, no. 2 (Summer 2004): 93–99.

10. *US/LEAP Newsletter*; O'Connor, interview; Villeda, interview; Coats, interview, July 26, 2004; Max Krochmal, "Sculpting Transnational Unionism."

11. For the IUF: www.iuf.org; "IUF and Chiquita Agreement on Freedom of Association, Minimum Labor Standards and Employment in the Latin American Banana Sector"; Coats, interview, July 26, 2004.

12. SiD calender; www.SiD.org; Munguía, interviews, November 18, 2002, and September 3, 2003; Zepeda, interview, November 13, 2002; "Delegación de Sindicalistas Daneses Visita COSIBAH," *Nueva Visión Sindical*, April 2002, 17.

13. José María Martínez, interview.

14. *Lo Que Hemos Vivido*, 11; COLSIBA, *Diagnóstico Participativo*, 10; Munguía, interview, September 3, 2003.

15. "Convenio, Centro de Solidaridad AFL-CIO y Coordinadora de Sindicatos Bananeros y Agroindustriales de Honduras COSIBAH; Proyecto: Activistas de Educación y Organización Sindical," COSIBAH Archives; Nuñez, interview; Lagos, interview, November 12, 2002.

16. Munguía, interviews, November 18, 2002, September 3, 2003, and September 1, 2004; Edilberta Gómez, interview, November 15, 2002; www. brot-fuer-die-welt.de.

17. On the role of NGOs in Latin American women's movements: Sonia Álvarez, "Advocating Feminism: The Latin American Feminist NGO 'Boom,'" *International Feminist Journal of Politics* 1, no. 2 (1999): 181–209; Álvarez, "Translating the Global"; Amrita Basu, "Globalization of the Local/

Localization of the Global: Mapping Transnational Women's Movements," in *Meridians: Feminism, Race, Transnationalism* 1, no. 1 (2000): 68–84 ; Manisha Desai, "Transnational Solidarity: Women's Agency, Structural Adjustment, and Globalization," in Nancy Naples and Manisha Desai, *Women's Activism and Globalization.*

18. *Lo Que Hemos Vivido,* 60.
19. Ibid.
20. Torres, interview.
21. Edilberta Gómez, interview, November 15, 2002.
22. Gloria García, interview, November 18, 2002.
23. *Lo Que Hemos Vivido,* 117.
24. Munguía, interviews, November 18, 2002, and September 3, 2004.

CONCLUSION

1. For an overview of women in the Central American labor movement: Naranjo Porras, *Diagnóstico Sobre Participatión*; and ORIT, *Mujer y Trabajo: Diagnóstico Sociolaboral y Sindical de America Latina y El Caribe* (Caracas, Venezuela: ORIT, 2002), in COSIBAH Archives.
2. Basu, "Globalization of the Local"; Basu, ed., *The Challenge of Local Feminisms: Women's Movements in Global Perspective* (Boulder, CO: Westview Press, 1995); Álvarez, "Translating the Global"; Álvarez, "Latin American Feminisms 'Go Global': Trends of the 1990s and Challenges for the New Millenium," in *Cultures of Politics/Politics of Cultures: Re-visioning Latin American Social Movements,* ed. Álvarez, Evelina Dagnino, and Arturo Escobar (Boulder, CO: Westview Press, 1998); Chandra Talpade Mohanty, *Feminism Without Borders: Decolonizing Theory, Practicing Solidarity* (Durham, NC: Duke University Press, 2003); Naples and Desai, *Women's Activism and Globalization*; Inderpal Grewal, "On the New Global Feminisms," in *Scattered Hegemonies: Postmodernity and Transnational Feminist Practices,* ed. Inderpal Grewal and Caren Kaplan, (Minneapolis: University of Minnesota Press, 1988); Valentine M. Moghadam, "Transnational Feminist Networks: Collective Action in an Era of Globalization," *International Sociology* 15, no. 1 (2000): 57–85.
3. For a discussion of the term *transnational*: Nancy A. Naples, "Changing the Terms: Community Activism, Globalization, and the Dilemmas of Transnational Feminist Praxis," in Naples and Desai, *Women's Activism and Globalization,* 8.
4. Too often "the labor movement" and "women's movements" are conceptualized as separate and nonoverlapping concepts. In analyses of Latin America (and elsewhere) this has been in part because of the labor movement's historical resistance to incorporating women as equals and addressing their concerns. See, e.g., Levenson-Estrada, "Working-Class Feminism"; Méndez, "Creating Alternatives from a Gender Perspective." For discussions of this question in contemporary Central America, with different interpretations of the intersection of class politics, the labor movement, and the women's movement: Stephen, *Women and Social Movements,* 2–3, and Méndez, "Creating Alternatives," 122. Basu, in "Globalization of the Local," 73, notes

of transnational women's movements: "A minority...seek to challenge the feminization of poverty and class inequality that globalization entails." It may be, rather, that scholars have been unaware of the extent of women's feminist/ gender activism in the labor movement—such as the banana women's. For a pathbreaking, parallel argument about the history of feminism in the United States, see Dorothy Sue Cobble, *The Other Women's Movement: Workplace Justice and Social Rights in Modern America* (Princeton, NJ: Princeton University Press, 2004). Cobble rewrites the history of twentieth-century US feminism to show how it didn't "disappear" in the 1940s and 50s but, rather, flourished within the labor movement.

5. *Lo Que Hemos Vivido*, 8.

6. Ibid., 64.

7. Anthony Carew, Michel Dreyfus, Geert van Goethern, and Rebecca Grumbell-McCormick, eds., *The International Confederation of Free Trade Unions* (Bern, Switzerland: Peter Lang, 2000); Peter Waterman, "The Problematic Past and Uncertain Future of the International Confederation of Free Trade Unions," *International Labor and Working-Class History*, no. 59 (Spring 2001): 125–32; for a discussion of new leadership and roles for the ICFTU: Kjeld Jakobsen, "Rethinking the International Confederation of Free Trade Unions and its Inter-American Regional Organization," in Peter Waterman and Jane Wills, *Place, Space and the New Labour Internationalisms* (Oxford: Blackwell, 2001): 59–79.

8. For discussions of new models of international labor solidarity, Waterman and Wills, *Place, Space*; Peter Waterman, *Globalization, Social Movements, and the New Internationalism* (London: Continuum, 2001); Michael E. Gordon and Lowell Turner, *Transnational Cooperation Among Labor Unions* (Ithaca, NY: ILR / Cornell University Press, 2000); Dale Hathaway, *Allies Across the Border: Mexico's "Authentic Front" and Global Solidarity* (Cambridge, MA: South End Press, 2000); Kim Moody, *Workers in a Lean World: Unions in the International Economy* (New York: Verso Books, 1998); Bruce Nissen, "Cross-Border Alliances in the Era of Globalization," in *The Transformation of U.S. Unions*, ed. Ray M. Tillman and Michael Cummings (Boulder, CO: Lynne Rienner, 1999); Bruce Nissen, *Unions in a Global Economy: International and Comparative Perspectives* (Toronto, ON: Thompson Educational, 2002); special issues of *Labor Research Review*, "Solidarity Across Borders: U.S. Labor in a Global Economy," no. 13 (1989), and "Confronting Global Power: Union Strategies for the World Economy" 23 (1995); Tim Shorrock, Mark Levinson, Subhashini Ali, Rachel Neumann, and articles on solidarity with Chinese labor by Anita Chan and Gregory Mantsios in "Labor and International Affairs," special section of *New Labor Forum* 11 (Fall/Winter 2002); Stanley Gacek, "Lula and Chavez: Differing Responses to the Washington Consensus," *New Labor Forum* 13, no. 1 (Spring 2004); Robert Collier, "Old Relationships Die Hard."

9. *Lo Que Hemos Vivido*, 78.

10. Ibid., 13.

Index

unions in, 4, 12, 62–63, 66, 98, 100
Education, 17, 41; union-based, 23, 27, 32, 38, 41
El Progreso, Honduras, 1, 30, 54
El Salvador, 5, 11, 29, 57, 58,
Euroban, 98
Europe, 6, 10, 38, 45, 63, 98–99, 102, 110
'Emilia' (pseudonym), 24, 28, 30, 91
Escuela Nacional Sindical (National Labor School), Colombia, 73
Facio, Alda, 97
Federación de Sindicatos Bananeros de Chinandega (Federation of Chinandega Banana Unions; FETRABACH), 64, 77, 79, 89, 100, 101
Federación Independiente de Trabajadores de Honduras (Independent Federation of Honduran Workers; FITH), 69–70
Federación Nacional de Campesinos e Indígenas Libres de Ecuador (National Federation of Farmers and Free Indigenous Peoples of Ecuador; FENACLE), 66
Feminism: Central American Left, 25; Honduran, 52; middle-class, 96–97; transnational, 5, 107
Flexible labor systems, 16, 69
Free trade agreements, 18, 62; *See also* CAFTA, FTAA
Free Trade Area of the Americas (FTAA), 69, 97
Frente Sandinista de Liberación Nacional (Sandinista National Liberation Front; FSLN), 11, 25
Funding, outside, 39, 75, 76, 82–83, 99–101
Funez, Juan, 69
Fyffes, 9, 10
Galindo, Oneyda, 54, 88, 89
Garay, Alirio Antonio, 44
García, Doris, 67

García, Gloria, 14; and SITRATERCO, 26, 29, 31, 32; and COSIBAH, 1–3, 44–45; and COLSIBA, 72, 77, 101
Gender, politics of: discussed in SITRATERCO, 27, 32; in COSIBAH: 3–4, 37, 41, 50, 51, 56; in COLSIBA, 97–98
Globalization, 42, 68–69
Gómez, Edilberta (Berta), 79, 89, 91, 101
Gómez, Telma, 62, 84
Grau Crespo, Ariane, 96, 107
Great Britain, 98
Guatemala, 2–4, 17–18, 29, 57, 78; and Hurricane Mitch, 31; unions in, 63, 64, 78; US support of 1954 coup, 11; women's union activism in, 2–4, 61, 64–65, 66, 67, 69, 72–73. *See also* Del Monte, kidnappings of unionists; SITRABI
Hanover, Germany, 102
Health care workers, 41, 52, 106
Health care, employer-paid, 13, 14, 15, 22, 41. *See also* Health and Safety, Pregnancy, Reproductive rights
Health and safety, workplace, 14–17, 41, 42, 68, 70
Hernández, Domitila, 1–3, 16, 42, 44, 72, 77
Hernández, Emilia, 76
Homosexuality, 91–92
Honduran Labor Code, 28, 46
Honduras, 4, 12, 31; COSIBAH and women's work in, 37–58; funding for unions in, 99–100; gender dynamics in, 88, 89, 92; Hondurans' participation in COLSIBA, 61, 67, 69, 72; salaries and working conditions in, 14–17; SITRATERCO and women's activism in, 21–54; special circumstances of, 57–58; women's movement in, 95–96;

ABOUT THE AUTHOR

DANA FRANK (top row, second from the right, with Nicaraguan and Honduran banana union activists at a FETRABACH workshop on domestic violence, Chinandega, Nicaragua, November 2004) is a professor of history at the University of California, Santa Cruz. Her books include *Buy American: The Untold Story of Economic Nationalism*; *Purchasing Power: Consumer Organizing, Gender, and the Seattle Labor Movement, 1919–1929*; *Local Girl Makes History: Exploring Northern California's Kitsch Monuments*; and *Women Strikers Occupy Chain Store, Win Big: The 1937 Detroit Woolworth's Strike*. Her writings on human rights and US policy in post-coup Honduras have appeared in the *New York Times, Los Angeles Times, Miami Herald, The Nation, Foreign Affairs, Foreign Policy, Politico Magazine, The Baffler*, and many other publications. She worked for many years with the US Labor Education in the Americas Project in support of the banana unions of Latin America.

ABOUT HAYMARKET BOOKS

Haymarket Books is a nonprofit, progressive book distributor and publisher, a project of the Center for Economic Research and Social Change. We believe that activists need to take ideas, history, and politics into the many struggles for social justice today. Learning the lessons of past victories, as well as defeats, can arm a new generation of fighters for a better world. As Karl Marx said, "The philosophers have merely interpreted the world; the point, however, is to change it."

We take inspiration and courage from our namesakes, the Haymarket Martyrs, who gave their lives fighting for a better world. Their 1886 struggle for the eight-hour day reminds workers around the world that ordinary people can organize and struggle for their own liberation.

For more information and to shop our complete catalog of titles, visit us online at www.haymarketbooks.org.

ALSO AVAILABLE FROM HAYMARKET BOOKS

China on Strike: Narratives of Workers' Resistance
Hao Ren, edited by Eli Friedman and Zhonhjin Li

Disposable Domestics: Immigrant Women Workers in the Global Economy
Grace Chang, foreword by Aijen Poo

Fields of Resistance: The Struggle of Florida's Farmworkers for Justice
Silvia Giagnoni

Lucy Parsons: An American Revolutionary
Carolyn Ashbaugh

Poor Workers' Unions: Rebuilding Labor from Below
Revised and Updated Edition, Vanessa Tait, forword by Bill Fletcher, afterword by Christina Tzintzún

Women Strikers Occupy Chain Store, Win Big: The 1937 Woolworth's Sit-Down
Dana Frank